THE QUIET
THAT RAISED ME

Shawn M. Mack

ATLAS ELITE
PUBLISHING

Published by **Atlas Elite Publishing Partners**
Cover design by **Michael Beas**

Ebook ISBN: 978-1-962825-97-9
Paperback ISBN: 978-1-962825-98-6

Printed in United States of America
For more information, visit:
www.atlaselitepublishingpartners.com

Table of Contents

Forgiveness Without Forgetting Yourself

Dedication

*For the people who stayed
and the ones who couldn't*

Chapter 1

When Safety Was Never Guaranteed

I wasn't just hurt; I was selected. In my house, anger didn't arrive to teach, guide, or correct. It hunted. It searched for release. And again and again, it found me. My stepfather's rage did not escalate logically or follow rules I could memorize. There was no formula, no obedience precise enough to keep me safe. It detonated without warning and sudden, explosive, violent and it left damage behind that was physical, overwhelming, and final. Safety was never a baseline. It was provisional. Fragile. Something that could be revoked without explanation or mercy.

Growing up inside that kind of danger rewires you at the root. You stop believing fairness offers protection. You stop asking why, because why does not stop impact. Answers do not soften fists. Logic does not deflect explosions. Slowly, every question collapses into a single imperative: how do I survive this?

Survival becomes the organizing principle of your existence. Not all at once. Gradually. Quietly. Until it governs how you enter rooms, how you sit in chairs, how you regulate your breathing. You learn to read tones before words are spoken. You measure the temperature of a space before stepping into it. You learn the difference between silence that means calm and silence that signals impending harm.

You also learn to manage other people's emotions as if your life depends on it—because sometimes it does. You monitor shifts. You adjust yourself in real time. You become smaller, quieter, sharper, faster. And when you fail, you pay.

People soften this by calling it discipline, but discipline has intention and proportion. What I lived under was domination. And domination corrodes a child's understanding of love in ways that do not fade. It teaches you that care and violence can inhabit the same body. That protection and terror can come from the same source. That attachment is never neutral, it is always a risk.

That confusion does not dissolve with time. It embeds. To be scapegoated is to be blamed before you even understand what blame is. It is to be assigned responsibility for emotional weight that was never yours to carry.

You become the container for someone else's fury, instability, and self-loathing. Your inner life becomes irrelevant.

Your pain becomes inconvenient. Peace does not mean safety. Peace means compliance. Peace means silence. Peace means learning exactly when to erase yourself.

Scapegoating breeds vigilance. You become hyper-attuned to emotional weather other people never notice a hesitation in footsteps, a shift in breath, the pressure under a sentence that sounds harmless to everyone else. Later, this sensitivity may be mistaken for intuition or emotional intelligence. But its origin is fear. Over time, you stop evaluating whether something is fair or deserved. Responsibility becomes reflexive. Guilt arrives before evidence. Self-blame becomes automatic.

Even when the bruises fade, the belief remains: if something goes wrong, it must be because of me. That belief does not stay locked in childhood. It follows you forward. It threads itself into identity. It shapes how you respond to conflict, how quickly you accept fault, how deeply you internalize responsibility for things you did not cause. It becomes the lens through which you see yourself not as someone reacting to harm, but as someone inherently responsible for it.

For many years, I didn't realize I was wearing a mask. It didn't feel like pretending. It felt like functioning. The mask was not deception. It was protection, assembled slowly, one adjustment at a time, out of sheer necessity. Beneath it lived a younger version of me who learned

3

early that showing need was dangerous, that softness invited impact, and that vulnerability could be weaponized. He learned to stay quiet. To stay alert. To stay hidden.

The mask became competence. Control. Intensity. Charm. Strength. Achievement. Independence. It worked. It carried me through rooms. It earned admiration. It produced results. It kept me alive in a world that rewarded performance and punished need. But it also built distance—first from others, then from myself. What I didn't understand for a long time was that the mask doesn't fall away when childhood ends. It calcifies. It evolves. It becomes convincing. The traits that once protected you begin to pass as personality. And because they are rewarded, they go unexamined.

Intimacy changes everything. When closeness enters the picture, the mask tightens instead of loosening. Intimacy demands openness, uncertainty, reliance of the exact conditions that once preceded danger. The body remembers this instantly. Old alarms ignite. Muscles brace. Control rushes in. The nervous system prepares for explosion even when no threat exists.

The reaction is swift, involuntary, and difficult to interrupt. This is the cruel paradox of survival: What once kept you alive can later imprison you. The child learned to endure. The adult learned to perform. And beneath both, a nervous system remained locked in anticipation of harm. Understanding this did not excuse the ways I later hurt people. It did not undo consequences. But it finally named what I had spent years condemning as personal failure. It gave language to reactions that always felt excessive, confusing, and out of proportion.

It revealed the truth beneath the mask: a child who learned very early that safety always came at a cost.

Healing, I came to understand, would not come from ripping that mask away. It would come from teaching the part beneath it—slowly, patiently, relentlessly—that the explosions were over. That hiding was no longer the price of survival. That safety no longer had to be earned by disappearing.

Chapter 2

When Survival Becomes Identity

Survival does not announce when it takes over. It does not arrive with a clear beginning or a moment you can point to later and say, this is when it happened. It slips in quietly, disguised as adaptation. At first, it is simply what you do to get through the day. Over time, it becomes who you are.

As a child, survival is situational. You learn what keeps you out of trouble, what draws attention, what invites danger, and what allows you to pass unnoticed. You learn how to read a room before you speak. You learn how to measure your presence, how much space you're allowed to take up, how to stay one step ahead of whatever might come next. None of this is deliberate. It is learned through repetition, through consequence, through the body registering what worked and what didn't.

But something subtle happens when danger is not temporary. The strategies that once helped you endure begin to organize your entire way of being. Survival stops being something you do and becomes something you are.

You no longer drop the posture when the threat passes, because the threat never clearly ends. The nervous system never receives confirmation that it is safe to stand down.

What makes this transition so difficult to recognize is that survival-based traits often look functional, even impressive. The child who learns to anticipate danger often grows into an adult who is observant, capable, and deeply attuned to others. Vigilance becomes perceptiveness. Self-control becomes discipline. Emotional restraint becomes maturity. Reliability becomes identity. These qualities are praised. They are rewarded. They become part of how others describe you.

No one asks what it costs to live that way.
Beneath the competence, the body remains organized around threat. It never stops scanning. It never fully rests. Even in moments that should feel calm, there is an undercurrent of readiness, a quiet tension that says something could still go wrong. The danger no longer needs to be present for the system to behave as if it is.
This is how survival becomes identity.

Trauma does not live only in memory. It lives in expectation. When a child grows up in an environment marked by unpredictability or violence, the body adapts by staying alert. Muscles hold tension without awareness. Breathing stays shallow.

Attention remains outward, monitoring tone, posture, and mood. This state becomes baseline. Over time, vigilance feels normal. Calm, by contrast, feels unfamiliar. Silence can feel dangerous. Ease can feel suspicious.

The body learns that staying ready is safer than relaxing. This conditioning persists long after the original threat is gone. It explains why people who grew up in unsafe environments often struggle to rest even when their lives appear stable. It explains why relaxation can feel uncomfortable, why stillness can feel empty or exposing, and why the nervous system resists slowing down. Endurance once meant survival. Letting go now feels like risk.

Living in this state has consequences that are easy to overlook at first. Constant readiness creates a low-level tension that never fully resolves. Uncertainty becomes intolerable. Ambiguity feels charged. Ordinary disagreements can trigger disproportionate reactions because the body learned long ago that conflict precedes harm. When tension appears, the system responds quickly, sometimes with withdrawal, sometimes with control, sometimes with intensity, sometimes with shutdown.

These responses are not chosen. They are reflexive.

The nervous system moves faster than conscious thought. By the time awareness arrives, the reaction has already happened.

Over time, these adaptations settle into what feels like personality. You begin to describe yourself in ways that sound neutral or even positive. You say you're intense, independent, perceptive, responsible, always prepared. None of these descriptions are false. They describe real patterns. What they don't reveal is why those patterns formed.

Hypervigilance can look like insight. Control can look like leadership. Emotional distance can look like strength. Self-reliance can look like confidence. Because these traits are often socially rewarded, they rarely raise concern. They function. They succeed. They keep life moving forward.

But identity built on survival narrows experience. It limits spontaneity. It makes rest feel unsafe. It turns connection into something that must be managed rather than received. Vulnerability becomes a liability. Need becomes something to hide.

There is a particular loneliness that comes with being seen as strong while feeling internally braced.

When others rely on you, expect you to hold things together, or admire your composure, it becomes harder to admit how much effort that composure requires.

Needs feel like burdens.
Asking for support can trigger shame.
Dependence feels like failure.

Over time, you may begin to treat yourself the same way you were once treated, with pressure instead of care, with criticism instead of patience. The internal voice becomes strict, demanding that you not falter, not need too much, not lose control. What began as an external threat becomes internal governance.

This is not discipline in its healthy form. It is self-surveillance.

The cost of survival-based identity becomes most visible in close relationships. Intimacy asks for presence rather than vigilance. It requires openness instead of monitoring. It involves uncertainty, mutual influence, and emotional risk. These are precisely the conditions that challenge the strategies that once kept you safe.

As closeness increases, old alarms activate. Emotional exposure feels dangerous. The urge to manage, control, or withdraw intensifies.

Reactions may feel confusing, even to the person having them. The desire for connection exists alongside a deep fear of what connection might cost.

This is not because intimacy is inherently unsafe. It is because the nervous system learned to associate closeness with risk.

Recognizing this pattern is not about blame. Survival-based identity forms for a reason. It reflects intelligence, adaptability, and resilience in the face of real conditions. But strategies designed for danger are not meant to govern a life indefinitely. When they become permanent, they begin to limit rather than protect.

Understanding this shift marks a turning point. It is the moment when the question changes from "what is wrong with me"? to "what happened to me and how did I adapt?" That question opens the door to compassion. Compassion opens the door to choose.

Healing does not require erasing who you became to survive. It begins by recognizing that identity shaped by danger can be reshaped by safety, slowly and deliberately. The survival self does not need to be destroyed. It needs to be understood, acknowledged, and taught that the conditions which created it no longer define the present.

Chapter 3

The Nervous System Under Threat

Long before a child has language for fear, the body learns it. Trauma does not begin as a story that can be told or remembered cleanly. It begins as sensation, as a tightening in the chest, a sharp intake of breath, a sudden alertness that arrives without explanation. The nervous system learns first. Understanding comes much later, if it comes at all.

The nervous system has one primary responsibility: to keep the body alive. When danger appears, it does not pause to consider context or intention. It mobilizes immediately. Heart rate increases. Muscles tense. Attention narrows. The body prepares to fight, flee, freeze, or appease, whichever response once reduced harm most effectively. For a child living with ongoing threat, this state does not resolve. It becomes baseline.

In environments marked by violence, volatility, or emotional danger, the body stops trusting that calm is safe. Rest feels provisional. Stillness feels exposed. Even moments of quiet carry an edge, as if something might arrive without warning. The system remains partially always activated, holding tension in places that go unnoticed until exhaustion sets in.

Over time, this state stops feeling like stress and starts feeling normal. The body adapts so completely that the person may not recognize they are living in constant defense. They may simply experience themselves as alert, driven, or unable to slow down. Calm can feel foreign. Ease can feel undeserved. Silence can feel heavy.

What makes trauma especially disorienting is that it does not remain in the past. The nervous system does not track time the way the mind does. It responds to cues, not dates. A tone of voice, a sudden movement, raised volume, emotional intensity, unpredictability—these signals can activate the same physiological response that once helped a child survive. The reaction happens before conscious thought has time to intervene.

This is why trauma responses often feel disproportionate in adulthood. A situation that is objectively safe can trigger a reaction shaped by much earlier danger. The body responds as if the threat is present because, in its memory, it is. The response is not about now. It is about then.

Once the nervous system associates certain cues with danger, it creates a loop that reinforces itself. A trigger appears. The body activates. Control or defense increases. Tension escalates.

Relief comes only after withdrawal, resolution, or collapse. The system learns that the cycle worked and stores it for future use. Each repetition strengthens the pattern.

Over time, this loop can shape behavior in ways that feel confusing and frustrating. Hypervigilance becomes constant. Emotional reactivity increases. Shutdown or withdrawal feels like relief. Over-control feels stabilizing. Uncertainty becomes intolerable. Conflict feels threatening. Calming down after stress takes longer and longer.

Because these responses are automatic, people often judge themselves harshly for them. They wonder why they overreact, why they can't let things go, why relationships feel so exhausting. What they don't see is that their nervous system is doing exactly what it was trained to do. It is not malfunctioning. It is executing a survival program that once made sense.

This is why logic alone rarely changes trauma responses. You can understand your history, recognize your patterns, and know intellectually that you are safe, and still feel activated. The nervous system does not respond to reasoning the way the mind does. It responds to experience, repetition, and safety over time.

Telling yourself to calm down often fails because calm was never something the body learned to trust. Reassurance may bounce off because the system learned long ago that words did not guarantee protection. Awareness helps, but it does not immediately rewire a body that learned through lived experience that danger could arrive without warning.

These conditioning shapes adult life in subtle but powerful ways. It can make people highly sensitive to shifts in mood or tone. It can create discomfort with ambiguity. It can drive constant preparation for worst-case outcomes. It can fuel overthinking and intense reactions to stress.

These are not character flaws.
They are adaptations.

But adaptations that remain unchecked can interfere with intimacy, trust, and emotional safety. They can turn closeness into threat and disagreement into danger. They can create a gap between intention and impact that leaves people confused about themselves and ashamed of reactions they don't fully understand.

Understanding the nervous system offers a different lens. It reframes behavior not as failure, but as information. It reveals that what feels broken is often deeply learned. And it points toward a different approach to healing.

Healing does not begin by forcing the nervous system to stop reacting. It begins by listening to it. The goal is not to eliminate survival responses, but to help the body learn that it no longer must live in constant defense. That rest is allowed. That closeness does not always lead to harm. That safety can be experienced gradually and repeatedly.

This process is slow. It requires patience and gentleness. It involves teaching the body, through experience, that the present is different from the past. That protection no longer must come at the cost of connection. That vigilance can soften without catastrophe.

The nervous system learned to protect you when no one else could. Healing begins when it learns it does not have to do that alone anymore.

Chapter 4

The Anger That Had Nowhere to Go

Anger does not disappear just because a child is not allowed to feel it. When a child is hurt and cannot fight back, cannot escape, and cannot protest without risking more harm, anger does not evaporate. It has nowhere to go. It sinks inward. It settles into the body. It waits.

In unsafe homes, anger is dangerous. It can provoke punishment. It can escalate violence. It can mark you as a problem. So the child learns quickly that anger must be hidden, denied, or swallowed whole. What remains visible on the outside is compliance or quiet endurance. What remains on the inside is pressure.

Anger is not cruelty. It is not aggression by nature. It is a boundary response, the body's signal that something is wrong, that a line has been crossed. It mobilizes energy to protect, to resist, to say no. When that signal cannot be expressed, it does not resolve. It becomes trapped.

For a child who is scapegoated, anger becomes especially dangerous. Blame already belongs to them before they speak. Any protest only confirms the role they have been assigned. Expressing anger does not lead to relief. It leads to more punishment. Suppressing it leads to internal harm. There is no safe option.

Over time, anger fuses with shame. The child learns not only that expressing anger is unsafe, but that feeling it at all is evidence of being bad. Anger becomes proof of defectiveness. The body learns to clamp down on it, to redirect it, or to turn it inward. This is how anger goes underground.

What is buried does not stay still. It adapts. It finds other ways to surface without being named. It shows up as tension held in the jaw, the shoulders, the stomach. It shows up as irritability, impatience, and rigidity. It shows up as control, emotional distance, sudden defensiveness, or a low-grade resentment that never fully resolves. It shows up as self-criticism so harsh it feels punishing.

These expressions feel safer than open anger. They do not invite immediate retaliation. But they come at a cost. The original protest remains unspoken. The injustice remains unacknowledged. The energy stays trapped in the body, accumulating over time.

Under stress, especially in close relationships, that pressure looks for release. It may surface suddenly, in moments that feel disproportionate or confusing. The reaction may feel like it came out of nowhere. It came from years of containment.

For someone who learned early that anger made things worse, this can be terrifying. They may fear their own intensity. They may work hard to appear calm, reasonable, or controlled. They may over-intellectualize their feelings or suppress them until they erupt. They may swing between silence and explosion, then collapse into regret.

None of this is a moral failure. It is what happens when a protective emotion is never allowed to develop safely. Anger, when unexamined, becomes dangerous not because it exists, but because it is misunderstood. When it is treated as something to eliminate rather than something to understand, it gains power. When it is fused with shame, it becomes volatile. When it is denied, it leaks out sideways.

Learning to relate to anger differently is one of the most destabilizing and necessary parts of healing. It requires unlearning the belief that anger itself is the problem. It requires separating the feeling from the behaviors that once followed it. It requires acknowledging that the anger made sense.

Anger points to violated boundaries. It signals where something was taken without consent. It marks places where needs were ignored, voices were silenced, or power was abused.

In childhood, these signals could not be acted on. In adulthood, they often surface indirectly, through urgency, tone, or reactivity.

This is where misunderstanding begins. A person may judge themselves harshly for feeling angry without recognizing that the anger is communicating something legitimate. Others may experience the anger without seeing the vulnerability beneath it. The result is distance, confusion, and often shame.

In some cases, anger becomes folded into the mask. It appears as intensity, certainty, or emotional armor. This version of anger feels safer than vulnerability. It keeps others at a distance. It protects the softer parts underneath. But it also limits connection. It narrows the emotional range. It reinforces the belief that closeness is risky.

Healing does not require acting anger out or pushing it down. It requires making space for it without letting it take control. That space begins with permission, permission to feel anger without shame, permission to name what was unfair, permission to acknowledge harm, permission to feel protective of the child who had no protection.

This is not about blame or revenge. *It is about truth.*

When anger is allowed to exist as information rather than threat, it begins to change. It becomes clearer. It becomes less explosive. It becomes something that can guide boundaries rather than break them. It restores a sense of agency that was once taken away.

For many survivors, learning to feel anger safely marks a turning point. It is the shift from helplessness to self-respect, from silence to internal alignment. It is the moment when the body is allowed to say, without apology, that what happened mattered.

That acknowledgment, steady and unflinching, becomes one of the foundations of real healing.

Chapter 5

Hypervigilance, Control, and the Illusion of Safety

When danger is unpredictable, the mind learns to stay ahead of it. Hypervigilance is not panic in the way people imagine. It is not frantic or obvious. It is quiet, constant, and exhausting. It is the background process that never shuts off, the internal radar that monitors tone, posture, timing, mood, and silence with equal intensity.

For a child raised in threat, vigilance is not optional. It increases the odds of survival. You learn to anticipate rather than react. You learn to notice what others miss. Over time, this scanning becomes automatic. Eventually, it stops feeling like fear at all. It feels like awareness.

Control often follows close behind.

When a child cannot control what is done to them, they learn to control everything else. Control becomes a substitute for safety. Planning, anticipating, managing, staying several steps ahead— these behaviors reduce uncertainty, and reduced uncertainty feels like relief. The nervous system confuses predictability with protection.

At first, control feels empowering. It creates order in a world that once felt chaotic. But control is effort. It requires constant attention.

It demands vigilance. Safety, by contrast, is passive. It allows rest. A nervous system shaped by trauma often does not recognize the difference.

Because hypervigilance and control often present as competence, they are reinforced. The person who is always prepared is praised. The one who notices everything is admired. The one who stays composed under pressure is trusted. What is rarely acknowledged is the cost of living this way.

The body remains in a low-grade state of alert. Muscles stay tense. Rest feels incomplete. Stillness feels uncomfortable. Uncertainty feels dangerous. Even moments of peace can feel strangely hollow, as if something is missing or about to go wrong.

Control becomes most complicated in close relationships. Intimacy introduces unpredictability. Another person brings their own emotions, needs, and rhythms. This variability can activate the same survival responses once used to manage danger. Control may show up as managing conversations, monitoring emotional shifts, needing reassurance, reacting strongly to perceived distance, or trying to stabilize the relationship through action rather than presence.

These behaviors are not about domination. They are about fear. They are attempts to reduce internal alarm. But even fear-driven control can strain connection. It creates pressure. It disrupts mutuality. It turns closeness into something tense rather than safe.

This is the illusion of safety. Control reduces anxiety temporarily, but it never resolves the underlying belief that danger is always near. When control slips, fear rushes back in. True safety feels different. It is not something you manage. It emerges when the nervous system learns that it no longer has to stay on guard.

Letting go of control does not mean becoming careless. It means learning to tolerate uncertainty without interpreting it as a threat. It means trusting that discomfort is not the same as danger. This learning cannot be rushed. It happens slowly, through repetition and experience.

Recognizing hypervigilance and control as survival strategies rather than character flaws is a turning point. These patterns kept you alive. They deserve acknowledgment, not condemnation.

Chapter 6

Why Intimacy Feels Dangerous

Intimacy is often described as closeness, safety, or connection. But for someone shaped by early danger, intimacy does not register as comfort. It registers as exposure. It feels like standing in open air without armor, like letting the door remain unlocked after years of learning that harm enters quietly. When a child grows up in an environment where closeness and pain coexist, the nervous system forms a brutal equation: proximity equals risk. What others experience as warmth, the body experiences as threat.

This association does not dissolve with time. It does not fade as language improves or maturity develops. It waits. It settles deep into the body and stays dormant until intimacy begins to deepen. Then it activates without asking permission. As connection grows, the body reacts before the mind can make meaning of it. A tightening spreads across the chest.

Breathing changes.
Thoughts accelerate.

The urge to regain control surges - through withdrawal, distraction, defensiveness, or sudden emotional distance.

Sometimes the impulse is subtle, barely noticeable. Sometimes it is overwhelming. Either way, it arrives without logic. And that is what makes it so destabilizing. The relationship may be wanted. The person may be valued. The connection may feel meaningful. And still, something inside begins to brace.

This is the central contradiction of trauma. The longing for closeness exists alongside a deep fear of it. A person can crave intimacy and simultaneously experience it as danger. They can move toward connection with hope, only to recoil once it starts to feel real. The nervous system does not distinguish between past and present. It recognizes sensation, not context.

Often this creates a push–pull pattern that feels maddening to live inside. At first, connection brings relief. It quiets loneliness. It offers warmth, validation, and a sense of being seen. But as emotional proximity increases—when attachment begins to solidify, when dependence becomes mutual, when loss becomes possible—old alarms ignite. The body prepares for an impact that may never come. Distance follows. Silence. Emotional retreat.

Hyper-analysis. Efforts to reestablish control. What once felt nourishing suddenly feels suffocating. The person experiencing this shift may not understand it. They may feel ashamed of it. They may tell themselves they are broken, avoidant, incapable of love. They may blame the other person for wanting too much or blame themselves for wanting too little. The body is responding to an old map - one drawn in an environment where closeness came with consequences.

Intimacy does not just activate fear. It activates memory. Early roles resurface without warning. The one who learned to manage others' emotions becomes hyper-attuned to a partner's moods, scanning for signs of withdrawal or anger. The one who learned that needs were dangerous struggles to ask for reassurance, even while desperately wanting it. The one who learned that conflict led to harm avoids disagreement at all costs - or reacts intensely when tension appears, because the body has no middle ground. These roles are not chosen. They emerge automatically when attachment systems come online. The body remembers what the mind may never consciously recall.

At the core of intimacy-related fear is not fear of love itself. It is fear of loss, fear of humiliation, fear of being exposed, and then abandoned. Closeness unconsciously carries meanings that were learned early and never updated: dependence equals danger, vulnerability equals punishment, love equals something that can disappear without warning. When intimacy deepens, it threatens to recreate a familiar wound, and the body moves to prevent that outcome by any means necessary.

Protective strategies once served a purpose. They preserved safety when safety was not guaranteed. They minimized harm when escape was impossible. But strategies that were adaptive in childhood can become destructive in adulthood. When they remain rigid, they interfere with connection. They create distance where closeness is desired. They sabotage relationships not out of indifference, but out of fear. Over time, this gap between longing and behavior leads to loneliness, frustration, and a particular kind of grief - the grief of wanting connection but not knowing how to stay inside it.

Understanding why intimacy feels dangerous changes the story. It replaces self-condemnation with context. It reframes withdrawal as protection rather than deflection. And it opens a path forward that does not involve forcing fear away or shaming the body into compliance. Healing asks for something slower and more demanding: teaching the nervous system, over time, that closeness does not always end in harm. That presence does not require collapse. That intimacy can exist without danger.

Only then does connection stop feeling like a threat - and begin to feel like something that can be held.

But they do not have to govern your life forever.

Chapter 7

When Protection Becomes Harm

Protection begins as wisdom. It is the body's quiet vow that what happened once will not be allowed to happen again. For a child who grew up unsafe, protection is not a preference or a strategy it is survival itself. It is the instinct that stands watch when no one else does. It is the small, frightened intelligence of a child learning how to endure what should never have been endured.

That protection was built for a reason. It was built to shield a little boy who had no power, no language, and no reliable safety. It learned to anticipate danger before it arrived. It learned to harden, to disappear, to control what could be controlled. It learned to read rooms, moods, and silences with precision because the cost of misreading them was too high. That protection kept him alive. It kept him functioning. It carried him forward when nothing else could.

But protection that never evolves eventually turns inward. What once guarded against harm can begin to create it.

This realization is one of the most painful moments in trauma recovery. To see that the very strategies that saved the child are now injuring the adult is a kind of grief all its own. It requires a level of honesty that dismantles comforting narratives. It forces a confrontation between intention and impact. Between the part that was trying to protect a wounded boy and the reality of the damage left in its wake.

Protection is reactive. It is not guided by values or clarity. It is governed by the nervous system. When a threat is perceived—accurately or not—the body acts first. Muscles tighten. Emotions retreat. Control asserts itself. Distance appears. Sometimes anger rises. Sometimes silence. These reactions are not choices made with reflection. They are reflexes shaped in moments when there was no time to think, only to survive.
But reflexes still have consequences.

In adulthood, protection becomes quieter but no less powerful. Hiding turns into emotional distance. Compliance turns into control. Silence turns into defensiveness. Freezing turns into withdrawal. These behaviors surface most often in moments that matter most—during closeness, during conflict, during emotional exposure. Precisely when presence is required, protection steps in and takes over.

From the inside, this feels like self-defense. Like preservation. Like preventing something terrible from happening again. The body believes it is guarding the same small boy it once had to save. But from the outside, it can feel cold. Confusing. Overwhelming. Hurtful. The person on the other side may feel shut out, pushed away, or suddenly alone.

And this is the unbearable paradox: protection meant to preserve connection begins to erode it.

Awareness rarely arrives in time. Patterns become visible only after something has been strained or lost. Only after distance has hardened into consequence. Only after the damage has landed.

And when that awareness comes, it is heavy with grief. Grief for the relationship. Grief for the harm caused without intention. And grief for the younger self who never had another option.

There is a particular sadness in realizing that the little boy inside was never the problem. He was never dangerous. He was never too much. He was wounded. He was afraid. And he learned to survive the only way he knew how. The tragedy is not that he protected himself. The tragedy is that no one ever taught him how to stop.

Responsibility begins here—not as punishment, not as self-destruction, but as agency. It means acknowledging impact without collapsing into shame. It means holding compassion for the origin of behavior while still taking ownership of its effects. It means no longer allowing fear to operate unseen and unchallenged.

Protection does not need to be eliminated. It needs to be updated. The nervous system must learn that the danger is no longer the same. That the child is no longer alone. That safety does not require withdrawal, control, or emotional disappearance. This learning is slow. It asks for pausing where reflex once ruled. For naming internal states instead of acting them out. For choosing responses that belong to the present, not the past.

When protection softens under awareness, it changes form. It becomes discernment instead of defense. It becomes a boundary instead of a barrier. It becomes care instead of control. And perhaps most importantly, it becomes a way of protecting the little boy inside without harming the life the adult is trying to build.

That is the work. And it is as sad as it is necessary.

Chapter 8

The Cost of Being Strong

Strength is celebrated without interrogation. It is praised as virtue, rewarded as character, admired as proof of resilience. From the outside, strength looks clean. Dependable. Impressive. It looks like composure under pressure, endurance without complaint, and the ability to keep going no matter what. For those shaped by early adversity, strength does not simply become a trait. It becomes an identity. And identities forged in survival always carry a cost that goes unacknowledged.

For a child growing up in an unsafe environment, strength is not aspirational. It is compulsory. There is no option to fall apart when no one is coming. No permission to rest when vigilance is required. No space for softness when softness invites danger. The child learns quickly—often without language—that survival depends on control. Emotional control. Behavioral control. Control over expression, over need, over reaction. Strength becomes the mechanism that keeps the world from collapsing further. This is not the strength of choice. It is the strength of necessity.

Over time, endurance hardens into self-definition. The child does not simply endure hardship; they organize themselves around it. They become observant. Capable. Self-sufficient beyond their years. They learn to anticipate problems before they arise, to manage emotions before they spill, to adapt before they are asked. They are praised for being "mature," "easy," and "independent." The adults around them feel relieved. The child seems fine. Strong. Handled.

But what looks like strength from the outside is often a nervous system locked in permanent self-protection.
As adulthood arrives, this survival-based strength is rewarded again. Employers rely on you. Friends lean on you. Partners admire your steadiness. You are the one who holds things together, who does not unravel, who shows up when others can't. And slowly—quietly—strength becomes a role you are expected to maintain. The world interprets your resilience as evidence that you don't need care. That you won't ask for much. That you will manage.

And you comply. Because you always have.

Over time, strength stops feeling empowering and starts feeling isolating. Vulnerability feels risky, not because closeness isn't desired, but because need feels unsafe. Asking for help feels like failure. Rest feels indulgent. Dependence feels dangerous.

You tell yourself you are fine even when exhaustion has sunk into your bones, even when your body is carrying far more than it was ever meant to hold.

Strength becomes emotional armor.

It contains pain. It prevents collapse. It keeps you functional. But armor is not neutral. Worn too long, it restricts movement. It dulls sensation. It blocks contact. What once protected you now interferes with intimacy. You begin to experience closeness as intrusion and care as something you must manage rather than receive. You want to be held, but your system doesn't know how to soften into it.

Self-reliance calcifies into rigidity. You handle everything yourself because relying on others feels unreliable, disappointing, or dangerous. You don't expect support, so you don't request it. You don't name needs, so no one learns how to meet you there. And eventually, the belief settles in quietly but firmly: if I don't do this alone, it won't get done.

Then the loss comes.

Not an abstract loss. Not a distant one. A loss that rips through the body and rearranges everything it thought it knew about strength.

Nearly two years ago, I lost my best friend.

He was strong in the way people admire without question. Big. Steady. Relentless in his dedication. A man who showed up for his family with presence and love that never wavered. A man whose loyalty was physical, visible, and unquestionable. Watching someone like that—someone built on commitment, purpose, and devotion—be dismantled by disease was unbearable. Cancer did not negotiate with his strength. It did not respect his discipline. It did not pause for the people who loved him. It took him piece by piece and left devastation in its wake.

Watching that happen tightened something inside me.

If someone that strong could be destroyed, what safety was left?

Grief did not soften me. It hardened me further. It reinforced the oldest belief: even the strongest fall, and when they do, no one is spared. The loss was so immense, so violent in its finality, that my system responded the only way it knew how—by retreating. By clenching. By pulling inward. I did not withdraw because I didn't care. I withdrew because caring felt too dangerous. Because attachment had once again proven catastrophic.

That loss didn't just break my heart. It confirmed my armor. The cost accumulated faster after that.

Exhaustion became baseline. Not the kind that resolves with sleep, but the deeper fatigue of always bracing for collapse. Needs became harder to identify because grief consumed so much internal space. Rest felt undeserved. Relationships strained under the weight of what I could not say. I carried sorrow silently, believing that strength meant not letting anyone see how deeply I was affected. Partners may have experienced distance without understanding why.

I was present, reliable, engaged—but no longer fully reachable. The strong one often feels unseen, not because they aren't valued, but because their effort has become invisible. Strength hides struggle so effectively that even you can lose access to it. And when overwhelm finally surfaces, shame rushes in. You've been strong for so long. What right do you have to falter now?

Healing asks for a different definition of strength.

- *Not endurance at any cost. But honesty.*
- *Not self-denial. But self-awareness.*
- *Not carrying everything alone. But allowing yourself to be supported.*

Letting go of survival-based strength does not mean becoming weak. It means updating a strategy that once saved you but now confines you. It means allowing gentleness where there was once only vigilance. It means acknowledging grief instead of armoring against it. It means letting yourself be human in places where you learned to be unbreakable.

And in that shift, something long denied becomes possible: rest without fear, closeness without armor, and a strength that no longer requires you to sacrifice yourself—or disappear—to maintain it.

Interlude

The Strongest Man I Knew

He was built like certainty.

The kind of man people lean on without asking if he can hold the weight. Big. Grounded. Tireless in his devotion. He loved his family out loud and without hesitation, the way only people with deep integrity do—through action, consistency, and presence. He showed up. He stayed. He carried responsibility like it was purpose, not burden.

Watching him get sick broke something fundamental in me.

Cancer did not arrive gently. It did not negotiate with his strength or respect his discipline. It dismantled him slowly and then all at once, stripping away pieces of a man who had never learned how to quit. I watched his body fail him while his loyalty never did. I watched someone who had spent his life protecting others become unable to protect himself from what was growing inside him.

There is a specific kind of horror in witnessing that.

Not just the loss, but the collapse of the belief that strength is enough.

He fought the way he lived. Quietly. Completely. Without spectacle. And still, it took him. It took his breath, his time, his future. It took him away from the people who needed him and from the life he had earned. It left devastation behind, raw, disorienting, permanent.

But the most unbearable part was not watching him disappear.

It was watching what his disappearance did to the person who loved him most.

I watched a woman who had built her life around him be crushed in real time. I watched devotion turn into shock, then into grief so heavy it altered her posture, her voice, the way she occupied space. I watched strength fail twice, once in his body, and again in the life that depended on it. The love between them did not protect her from devastation. It only deepened it.

That image lodged itself inside me.

When he died, something in me locked shut. I did not just grieve him. I absorbed the message. If someone that strong could be destroyed, and if love that real could still end in ruin, then safety was an illusion.

Permanence was a lie.

Attachment was a liability. Loving deeply meant agreeing to devastation you could not outrun. My nervous system took that conclusion as fact and responded the only way it knew how, by tightening its grip on everything.

I became quieter after that. More guarded. Less willing to lean. I carried the loss alone, telling myself I was honoring him by staying functional. By not collapsing. By doing what strong men do when there is no room to fall apart.

But strength did not protect him. And it did not protect her.

And it did not protect me.

His death did not make me softer. It made me afraid. Afraid to attach. Afraid to need. Afraid to open something that could be taken without warning. I withdrew not because I didn't care, but because caring had just proven catastrophic.

And that withdrawal did not stay contained. It followed me home.

It entered the place where closeness mattered most.
It settled between me and the person I was building a life with.

I did not pull away because love was gone. I pulled away because love suddenly felt dangerous. Because I had just watched devotion fail twice, once in the body of the man I admired, and once in the life of the woman left behind. Because my body believed that if I stayed too open, if I leaned too fully into connection, I would watch everything I loved be dismantled again.

So I armored myself where I should have stayed present.
I chose silence where I should have spoken.
I withdrew where I should have reached.

I thought I was protecting what mattered most.

I did not yet understand that protection can become harm. There are losses that teach you how fragile life is. And there are losses that teach you how fragile love is. And then there are losses that teach you how fragile you are. This was all three.

I still carry him with me, not as inspiration, not as motivation, but as a wound that never fully closes. As proof that devotion does not guarantee survival. As the moment my armor thickened, quietly, without my consent.

The Quiet That Raised Me

I lost my best friend.

And with him, I lost the illusion that strength can save the people we love and the ability, for a time, to stay open with the one I loved most.

Chapter 9

The Search for Recognition

One of the quietest and most misunderstood consequences of childhood sexual abuse is a hunger that rarely names itself clearly. It does not always look like desire. It does not always move toward sex. Often, it disguises itself as restlessness, as longing, as a persistent ache that feels emotional rather than physical. It is the hunger to be seen—to be recognized without being harmed.

When a child is violated, something foundational fractures. The experience of being acknowledged safely—to be noticed without being taken from, to be seen without being invaded—becomes distorted. Attention stops feeling neutral. Affection becomes unpredictable. Visibility carries risk. The nervous system absorbs this lesson not as memory, but as instinct: being seen can cost you.

That lesson does not eliminate the need for recognition. It intensifies it.

Human beings are wired to be mirrored. To be known. To feel that their inner world registers in someone else's awareness. When recognition is offered safely, it supports coherence, identity,and self-trust. When it is paired with harm, the need does not disappear—it becomes complicated. Charged. Urgent and frightening at the same time.

For survivors of abuse, recognition can begin to feel synonymous with existence itself. Being seen becomes proof that you matter. That you are real. That you are not invisible. But safety and recognition were never paired cleanly. Being noticed once came with threat. Being acknowledged once involved loss of agency. And so adulthood inherits a painful contradiction: the need to be seen remains powerful, while trust in closeness remains fragile.

This tension often splits a person internally.

One-part longs deeply for connection, affirmation, and acknowledgment. Another part fears exposure, dependence, and vulnerability. The body remembers too much. The nervous system stays alert. The mind tries to negotiate a solution that allows recognition without danger.

The digital world offers one.

Online spaces create connections without proximity. Visibility without full exposure. They allow identity to be curated, disclosure to be controlled, and distance to remain intact. For someone whose early experiences taught them that closeness is risky, this can feel safer than being fully known in real time. Attention can be received without complete presence. Emotions can be expressed selectively. Validation can arrive without immediate consequence.

This is not manipulation. It is adaptation.

When validation arrives, it can feel regulating. Being admired, noticed, or acknowledged can temporarily quiet long-standing shame and soothe an overactivated nervous system. For someone who grew up without consistent affirmation, that relief can feel profound. Stabilizing. Like oxygen. And because the relief is real—even if temporary—the nervous system learns to seek it again.

But external validation does not last. Its effects fade. The hunger returns. And when the need for recognition has never been met internally, the search often resumes externally—not out of deceit, but out of survival. The body is seeking regulation from an ache it never learned how to soothe from within.

Secrecy often enters quietly at this stage. Not as intention, but as fear.

Fear of being misunderstood.
Fear of judgment.
Fear of conflict.
Fear of losing connection.

When honesty once led to harm, concealment can feel protective. Emotional distance can feel safer than full exposure. A person may tell themselves they are avoiding unnecessary pain, not creating harm. But secrecy carries weight. What begins as self-protection can evolve into deception. What begins as coping can turn into behavior that wounds others.

This is where internal conflict deepens.

A person may genuinely care about their partner and still hide parts of themselves. They may long for closeness while avoiding the vulnerability it requires. They may feel deep remorse while not fully understanding the forces driving their behavior. This contradiction is painful.Confusing. And often soaked in shame.

Understanding this pattern does not excuse harm. But it does explain how harm can occur without malicious intent. Accountability does not begin with self-condemnation. It begins with clarity—seeing the unmet need beneath the behavior and taking responsibility for its impact.

Healing requires holding two truths at once: that harm occurred, and that the need beneath it was real. Growth lives in that tension. It asks for honesty without collapse, responsibility without self-destruction, and recognition that true repair begins not with punishment, but with understanding.

The search for recognition does not end when it is shamed away. It ends when it is met safely— first internally, then relationally. When visibility no longer feels dangerous. When being seen no longer requires fragmentation. When connection is allowed to exist without secrecy.

And in that integration, something profound becomes possible: recognition that no longer needs to be chased, validation that no longer depends on concealment, and a self that no longer must split in order to survive being seen.

Chapter 10

The Gap Between Intention and Impact

One of the hardest truths to face in healing is that good intentions do not prevent harm. Many people shaped by early trauma do not want to hurt anyone. They care deeply. They value loyalty. They want connection. They want to be good. And yet, despite these intentions, harm still occurs.

This is where the gap opens the space between what we mean and what happens.

Intention lives inside the mind. It reflects desire, motive, and self-concept. Impact lives in the world. It is how actions land on others, regardless of what was meant. The two are connected, but they are not the same.

For someone shaped by early trauma, this distinction can feel threatening. Being told that harm occurred can activate old narratives of blame and punishment. The nervous system reacts quickly. Shame floods the body. Defensiveness follows, not because of lack of care, but because survival wiring interprets accusation as danger. This is why conversations about impact can feel destabilizing.

They touch neural pathways formed long before language—pathways shaped by fear, punishment, and powerlessness. The body prepares to protect itself before understanding has a chance to settle.

But understanding does not erase responsibility. It makes responsibility possible.

Responsibility without understanding collapses into shame. Understanding without responsibility collapses into avoidance. Healing requires both. It asks a person to stay present with discomfort long enough to recognize impact without annihilating themselves in the process.

Often, awareness arrives late. Patterns that were invisible in real time become painfully clear in hindsight. Relationships are reinterpreted. Words spoken or withheld take on new weight. The cost of survival becomes visible.

This stage can be devastating. It carries grief, regret, and a sense of "if only I had known." That grief deserves space. It does not mean growth came too late. It means growth came when the nervous system could finally tolerate truth.

Accountability rooted in compassion allows a person to hold complexity.

To say: I was shaped by experiences I did not choose, and I am responsible for how I show up now. This balance is what allows growth without collapse.

Not all harm can be repaired. Insight does not guarantee reconciliation. Some losses remain. But internal repair still matters. Learning from the past changes the future. Growth does not erase what happened. It prevents repetition.

Chapter 11

Regret Without Self-Destruction

Regret does not arrive all at once. It seeps in. It finds you in quiet moments, in the space between thoughts, in the places where distraction used to live. It arrives after the body has finally slowed down enough to feel what it spent years outrunning. And when it comes, it does not ask permission.

For much of my life, survival moved faster than reflection. There was always something to manage, something to anticipate, something to endure. Regret requires stillness, and stillness once felt dangerous. It wasn't until the noise quieted that the weight of what had happened — and what I had done, began to settle.

Regret carries images. Moments replayed with new understanding. Words that could have been spoken but weren't. Silences that felt safer at the time and devastating later. It carries the knowledge that awareness came after impact, not before. That insight arrived only once the damage was already done.

For someone shaped by trauma, regret can feel especially punishing. It does not exist alone; it arrives braided with shame, with self-blame, with the old belief that if something went wrong, it must be because of me. The mind searches for a sentence severe enough to match the pain. The inner judge wakes up and sharpens its voice. It is tempting to turn regret into self-destruction. To believe that suffering is proof of accountability.

If the pain is intense enough, it somehow balances the scale. For a long time, I confused punishment with responsibility. That confusion made sense. In childhood, taking the blame often reduced danger. If I absorbed the fault, maybe the storm would pass.

But regret is not meant to be a weapon turned inward. It is meant to be a signal. It marks the moment when empathy has expanded enough to see what was once invisible.

Regret says: I understand now.
Self-destruction says: I am nothing but what I did.

Those are not the same.

True regret does not erase the self. It deepens it. It brings grief — not only for what was lost, but for who I was when I did not yet know how to do better.

It brings sorrow for the pain carried by others, and for the version of myself who did not yet have the tools to respond differently.

There is grief in realizing that insight came too late to save what mattered most. That awareness does not guarantee repair. That some doors close permanently. This grief is heavy, and it deserves to be felt without being turned into a verdict on one's worth.

Learning to hold regret without collapsing into self-hatred is one of the hardest forms of maturity. It requires sitting with the truth without annihilating the self. It asks for the courage to say: I see what I did, I feel the weight of it, and I am still here.

Regret, when held honestly, becomes a teacher. It sharpens attention. It changes how carefully one listens, how deliberately one speaks, how responsibly one shows up. It does not erase the past, but it reshapes the future. That is its purpose.

The work is not to eliminate regret, but to let it transform rather than destroy. To let it become wisdom instead of a life sentence. To allow remorse to coexist with dignity.

That balance is not easy. But it is where healing begins to deepen.

Chapter 12

Shame, Self-Hatred, and the Inner Judge

Shame is quieter than people expect. It does not usually arrive as a scream. It does not always announce itself through dramatic self-loathing or visible collapse. More often, it whispers. It settles into the background of thought and posture, and tone. It disguises itself as reason, as discipline, as moral clarity. It sounds responsible. It sounds adult. It says you should have known better. It says you always do this. It says this is who you are. And because it speaks calmly, because it speaks consistently, it is often mistaken for truth.

For many people shaped by early trauma, shame forms long before conscious self-awareness ever has a chance to develop. It grows in environments where blame is unpredictable, where safety is conditional, where love is withdrawn without explanation, and anger arrives without warning. In those environments, a child does not have the power to make sense of what is happening externally.

They cannot name abuse, neglect, or dysfunction. They cannot locate responsibility accurately. So, the mind does what it must to survive. It turns inward. If something is wrong, it must be me. That belief is not born of self-hatred at first. It is born of necessity. It offers a fragile sense of order. It creates an explanation where none exists. It gives chaos a reason and suffering a cause.

Over time, that belief hardens. It stops being a conclusion and becomes an assumption. And eventually, it becomes a voice.

The inner judge is not a conscience. It is not wisdom. It is not morality. It is a survival mechanism. It learned early that self-criticism could function as protection. If I stay ahead of my flaws, maybe I can prevent punishment. If I find what is wrong with me first, maybe I can fix it before someone else uses it against me. If I punish myself preemptively, maybe it will hurt less when the world inevitably does. The inner judge believes vigilance equals safety. It believes harshness equals control. And because it once served a purpose, it feels justified.

With repetition, the voice grows stronger. It monitors everything. Tone. Desire. Impulse. Expression. Mistake. It scans constantly for evidence of defectiveness. It narrates failures in vivid detail and minimizes progress until it barely registers. It reframes learning as proof of inadequacy and growth as something accidental or unearned. And because this voice formed early, before choice or context were available, it does not feel learned. It feels inherent. It feels like identity.

This is what makes shame so powerful. It does not feel like something you experience. It feels like something you are.

Shame differs from guilt in a critical and often misunderstood way. Guilt says something went wrong. Shame says I am wrong. Guilt points to behavior. Shame collapses the self into defectiveness. Guilt can motivate repair, accountability, and growth. Shame does not seek resolution. It seeks erasure. When shame dominates, change becomes nearly impossible because the self is experienced as fundamentally flawed rather than temporarily misaligned.

Living under the rule of the inner judge is exhausting. Joy feels undeserved, as if pleasure must be justified or postponed. Rest feels irresponsible, as though stopping invites punishment or failure. Vulnerability feels dangerous, not because connection isn't desired, but because exposure has historically carried consequences. Even accountability becomes distorted. When shame is in control, reflection becomes prosecution. Regret becomes evidence. Responsibility turns into self-attack. The goal is not repair. The goal is punishment.

When mistakes occur, the inner judge seizes them immediately. Past failures are pulled forward and lined up as proof. Context is stripped away. Growth is ignored. The internal courtroom is always in session, and the verdict is predetermined. You are guilty. You always have been. And because the voice is familiar, because it has been present for so long, it sounds convincing. It sounds like honesty. It sounds like realism.

But familiarity is not truth.

Understanding the origin of the inner judge changes the relationship to it. Healing does not begin by silencing the voice or arguing it into submission. That often backfires. The inner judge does not respond to force because it was built to respond to threat.

Healing begins with recognition.
With understanding its function.

With seeing that this voice once believed it was protecting you. It believed criticism could prevent harm. It believed vigilance could create safety.

Acknowledging that intention does not mean agreeing with the message. Gratitude for survival does not require obedience to outdated strategies.

There is a crucial distinction between self-responsibility and self-hatred, though they are often confused. Responsibility says I am accountable for my actions, and I am capable of change. Self-hatred says I am irredeemable. Responsibility invites learning. Self-hatred invites paralysis. One supports growth. The other collapses possibility. The inner judge thrives in that confusion, convincing you that cruelty toward yourself is the same thing as integrity.

Learning to interrupt automatic self-attack takes time. It requires patience and repetition and an entirely different posture toward the self. Instead of condemnation, curiosity becomes the intervention. Instead of asking what is wrong with me, the question shifts to what was happening inside me when this occurred. What need was unmet? What fear was activated? What old pattern was driving this response? This shift does not excuse harm or avoid accountability. It contextualizes behavior so that accountability can actually lead somewhere.

That shift creates space. And in that space, shame begins to loosen its grip. The inner judge no longer controls the entire narrative. The self becomes more than a list of failures. Possibility returns. Growth becomes accessible again. And slowly, quietly, something revolutionary begins to happen. You start relating to yourself not as a problem to be punished, but as a human being to be understood.

Chapter 13

When Seeking Validation Becomes a Betrayal

There are truths that arrive only after the damage is done. For me, one of the hardest was recognizing how my hunger to feel seen — shaped by early trauma and reinforced by years of emotional survival — contributed to the loss of the relationship I valued most.

I did not intend to betray someone I loved. I did not wake up wanting to cause harm. But intention does not erase impact. And understanding that distinction has been one of the most painful reckonings of my life.

Before there was secrecy, there was distance. Not a lack of care, but a lack of safety. Fear made closeness feel dangerous. Vulnerability felt like exposure. Instead of naming that fear, I withdrew. I became guarded. Less present. Less open. Conversations flattened. Emotional availability thinned.

At the same time, the need to feel seen did not disappear. It looked elsewhere.

Validation arrived without risk. Without full presence. Without the vulnerability intimacy demands. The distance felt safer. The affirmation felt regulating. And slowly, almost imperceptibly, a split formed — one part maintaining the relationship, another seeking reassurance beyond it.

Even without physical boundaries being crossed, trust eroded. Emotional implications carry weight. Impact does not require intention to be real. Facing that truth required letting go of defensiveness and sitting with the pain of knowing that my coping strategies caused harm. Trauma does not excuse betrayal. But it explains how avoidance, fear, and unmet needs can intersect in destructive ways. Understanding this does not absolve responsibility. It deepens it.

Taking responsibility meant naming the harm without erasing my humanity. It meant acknowledging that fear led me away from alignment with my values. It meant accepting consequences without collapsing into self-hatred.

Some losses cannot be undone. Some relationships do not survive delayed awareness. That grief is real. But meaning can still be made from it. Living differently going forward becomes a way of honoring what was lost without rewriting the past.

Chapter 14

When Protection Looks Like Selfishness

One of the hardest realizations I faced was this: there were moments when my actions looked selfish, even though they were driven by fear.

From the outside, it could appear that I prioritized myself — my comfort, my needs, my protection. And in a way, I did. But what guided me was not entitlement. It was survival. It was a nervous system acting as if danger were still present long after it had changed shape.

Fear narrows focus. When fear takes over, partnership fades into the background. The question is no longer what is best for us, but how do I get through this moment without falling apart?

From the outside, that looks like withdrawal. Avoidance. Inconsistency. From the inside, it feels like self-preservation.

Understanding this distinction does not erase harm. But it explains how fear can masquerade as selfishness. I was not choosing against my partner. I was failing to choose with them.

That realization was devastating. Because it meant acknowledging that love alone was not enough. That intention was not enough. That protection, left unexamined, became destructive.

Taking responsibility meant naming that truth without turning it into a weapon against myself. Responsibility is steadier than shame. It allows ownership without annihilation.

Protection does not need to disappear. It needs to evolve. It needs to learn that safety no longer requires distance, secrecy, or control. That vulnerability does not automatically lead to harm.

This evolution is slow. It requires awareness, patience, and humility. It asks for the courage to pause when fear arises and to choose presence instead of reflex.

I was not acting from who I wanted to be. I was acting from what I feared. Naming that truth did not undo the past. But it changed how I step into the future.

And that — choosing integrity over defense, presence over fear — is where healing begins to move forward.

Chapter 15

Grief, Withdrawal, and the Weight That Followed

There are moments when life doesn't simply test your coping. It crushes it. It takes whatever fragile balance you've built between functioning and feeling and snaps it clean in half. And if your nervous system has already been shaped by danger, by unpredictability, by having to survive what you should never have had to survive, grief does not arrive like a visitor.

It arrives like a flood.

When someone I loved deeply died, something in me did not just break. It caved in. It wasn't only sadness. It wasn't only missing them. It was the violent rearranging of my internal world. It was the sudden realization that life can take what matters most without warning and without negotiation. And the part of me that had once learned to brace for impact as a child didn't interpret this as loss.

It interpreted it as confirmation.

It confirmed the belief that love is dangerous because love can be taken. That attachment is risky because it makes you vulnerable. That if you let someone inside, you are handing life a weapon it can use against you.

I didn't think those words consciously. I didn't sit down and decide, now I will fear love. It happened in my body first. The heaviness arrived and settled into my shoulders, into my chest, into the way I moved through the day as if the air had thickened. The effort it took to do simple things multiplied. Getting out of bed became an act of will. Answering messages felt like lifting something heavy. Holding a conversation required oxygen I didn't feel like I had.

And then something else happened, quietly at first. The instinct to withdraw, already familiar, grew teeth.

Grief did not create my patterns. It intensified them. It took what was already there—my tendency to retreat when overwhelmed, my reflex to manage pain privately, my fear of being too much—and it amplified it until it became the only language I could speak.

At first, withdrawal felt like rest. Like self-preservation. Like hiding in a room when the house is on fire and you don't know where the exits are. I told myself I needed space. I told myself I was processing. I told myself I didn't want to burden anyone. I told myself I was protecting the people I loved from my darkness.

But the truth was harsher.

I didn't know how to be seen in grief.

Grief is exposing. It strips away polish. It pulls you into the raw parts of yourself that you cannot perform your way out of. And performance had been my lifeline. Competence. Strength. Holding it together. Being the one who endures. Being the one who doesn't fall apart.

Grief demanded that I fall apart. And instead, I tried to disappear.

It started with small things. A delay in returning a call. A message left unanswered. A conversation kept shallow because I couldn't tolerate depth. A smile that didn't reach my eyes. A laugh that felt borrowed. A nod when I wasn't listening because my mind was somewhere else, stuck in memory and absence, and the sudden fear that everything I loved could vanish again.

The world began to shrink.

Depression is not always crying. Sometimes depression is the dimming of everything. The dulling of color. The muffling of joy. The way your favorite song sounds like noise. The way food tastes like texture instead of comfort. The way even sunlight feels like an obligation.

It is the slow draining of life's meaning.
And when your world shrinks internally, connection starts to feel like a demand you can't meet. People think depression is sadness. For me, it was more like distance.

Fog. A thick internal wall that separated me from everything that used to matter, including the people I loved.

From the outside, it looked like I was disengaging. Like I was pulling away. Like I didn't care. Like I was choosing isolation.

Inside, it felt like I was sinking, and every attempt to reach outward felt like trying to swim through wet concrete.

What made it more complicated was that grief didn't exist alone. It activated everything beneath it. Old fear. Old wiring. Old beliefs. The part of me that had learned early that closeness can be dangerous took the loss as a warning sign. It began to interpret connection as risk. It began to move as if the only way to avoid future pain was to reduce attachment in the present.

Connection leads to loss.

That message, once learned in childhood through pain, resurfaced in adulthood through grief. And the nervous system didn't care that I was grown now. It didn't care that I had language, insight, awareness. It remembered its rule and it enforced it.

So I pulled inward.

And while I was pulling inward, someone I loved was watching me disappear.

This is where grief becomes dangerous in relationships. Not because grief is wrong, but because grief can erode capacity. It can make presence feel impossible. It can make communication feel exhausting. It can make emotional availability feel like standing in a storm without shelter.

A trauma-shaped nervous system does not ask for help when overwhelmed. It goes quiet. It goes inward. It goes away.

Withdrawal becomes protection. But protection has a cost.

Because the person on the other side of withdrawal does not experience it as protection. They experience it as absence. They experience it as rejection. They experience it as a door slowly closing without explanation.

And the hardest part is that both experiences can be true at the same time.

The Quiet That Raised Me

Inside, I was overloaded. Outside, I looked uninterested.
Inside, I was drowning. Outside, I looked distant.
Inside, I was trying not to collapse. Outside, it felt like I
didn't care.

I did care. I cared deeply.

But caring is not the same as being present.

Grief is heavy, and when it goes unspoken, it becomes heavier. Loss sits beside older wounds. Pain stacks on pain. Silence piles up like bricks. Eventually, the nervous system becomes overloaded, and withdrawal can feel like the only thing left that still works.

I didn't withdraw because I wanted to hurt anyone.

I withdrew because I did not know how to carry pain openly.

And looking back, I can see how grief intensified what was already fragile in me. It deepened emotional distance. It magnified avoidance. It made hiding feel like survival.

I can also see how that hiding caused harm. Both truths exist.

Acknowledging grief does not erase responsibility. But it adds context. It prevents the story from becoming simplistic. It replaces moral judgment with human reality: a person can be grieving and still be accountable for the way they treat the people who love them.

There is no purity in pretending grief didn't affect me. And there is no integrity in using grief as an excuse for distance.

The mature truth lives in holding both. I was grieving, and I withdrew.

That withdrawal had consequences. I see that now.
And seeing it does not undo the past, but it changes how I live forward. It changes the way I understand absence. It changes the way I interpret silence. It changes the way I relate to pain.

Grief will always be part of the story. It does not have to define its ending.

Chapter 16

When the Brakes Failed

There is a particular kind of horror in watching yourself do something you know is wrong and feeling unable to stop. It is not the horror of ignorance. It is the horror of awareness without control. The horror of witnessing your own momentum. The horror of realizing that insight, no matter how clear, does not automatically translate into capacity.

Looking back, the best way I can describe that period is this: it felt like being inside a runaway truck.
Not because I wanted destruction. Not because I was chasing chaos. But because once the speed increased, once the patterns started moving, once survival took the wheel, I didn't know how to slow it down. I could feel the danger. I could feel the cliff approaching. I could feel the damage accumulating.

And still, I kept moving.

Trauma does not always show up as panic. Sometimes it shows up as acceleration. As compulsion. As the inability to tolerate discomfort without reaching for relief.

As the automatic execution of old strategies even when those strategies are now harming everything you claim to value.

From the outside, it looks like choices. From the inside, it feels like inevitability.

This is one of the most misunderstood aspects of trauma-driven behavior: it can look intentional while feeling out of control. There is action, but not freedom. There is movement, but not agency. There is behavior, but not presence.

When the nervous system is overwhelmed, the pause collapses.

The space between impulse and action shrinks until it becomes almost nonexistent. The ability to reflect, to weigh consequences, to course-correct weakens. And what remains is urgency.

Urgency is not desire. Urgency is not truth. Urgency is the body screaming, reduce this distress now.

In that state, even destructive behavior can feel like relief. Not because it aligns with values, but because it temporarily quiets internal chaos. It becomes a release valve. A pressure drop. A momentary sedative.

That doesn't make it right.

But it explains why stopping can feel impossible in the moment.

Once momentum begins, it reinforces itself. Each action creates fallout. Fallout creates shame. Shame creates fear. Fear creates more urgency. Urgency creates more action. The cycle accelerates downhill like a vehicle gaining speed with every second.

At a certain point, even your attempts to stop become part of the chaos. You panic. You try to fix things mid-motion. You overcorrect. You promise things you can't sustain. You grasp for control while the internal system is already in survival mode.

And this is the cruelest part: you often know you're making it worse.

But the part of the brain that makes long-term decisions goes offline under stress. The body is no longer consulting your values. It is consulting your most primitive wiring. Fight. Flight. Freeze. Appease. Distract. Escape. Anything that lowers distress quickly.

So later, after the crash, the question haunts you. Why didn't I just stop?

The honest answer is brutal: because at that point, the system running the show was not equipped to stop. Not without help. Not without support. Not without skills that weren't yet built.

Insight does not equal control.

Awareness does not automatically restore the brakes.

And when the crash comes, it comes with consequences that don't care how much you regret the speed. Relationships fracture. Trust collapses. Loss becomes unavoidable. The damage becomes visible in full daylight.

And the clarity that follows is devastating.

Because now you see everything. The pattern. The choices. The impact. The moments where you could have asked for help and didn't. The moments where you could have been honest and weren't. The moments where you prioritized relief over integrity.

The weight of that realization can flatten a person.

This is the moment where shame tries to take over completely. It tries to rewrite your identity as your worst actions. It tries to convince you that remorse is meaningless because the damage is already done. It tries to push you toward self-destruction as if punishment is the only form of accountability.

But accountability after the crash is not about suffering. It is about recognition.

Recognizing warning signs earlier. Recognizing triggers sooner. Recognizing your limits before you exceed them.

Recognizing the moment, you are not safe inside yourself. Recognizing that you cannot out-willpower a nervous system that is dysregulated.

It takes humility to say: I needed help long before things fell apart. Not as an excuse. As an honest assessment. Healing is learning where the brakes live.

They do not live in perfection. They do not live in strength as performance. They live in regulation. Support. Boundaries. Honest communication. Learning to pause. Learning to tolerate discomfort without escaping. Learning to name what is happening internally before it becomes behavior.

That is what "brakes" are in a trauma-shaped life. They are not a switch.

They are a practice.

And it is possible to hold all of this at once: that harm occurred, that responsibility matters, that trauma played a role, and that change is still possible.
That is not denial. That is integration.

Chapter 17

The Quiet Ways Distance Hurts

Not all harm is loud.

Some harm is silent.

It arrives in the absence of what isn't said. In what is withheld. In the slow erosion of intimacy that happens when someone is technically present but emotionally gone.

I didn't explode, I didn't yell, I didn't make my pain obvious. What I did was withdraw.

I became shorter. I became quieter. I became harder to reach. I stayed busy. I stayed distracted. I stayed "fine." I kept the surface smooth while the inside of me drifted farther away.

Emotional withdrawal is one of the most deceptive forms of harm because it doesn't look like aggression. It looks like fatigue. It looks like stress. It looks like a person who is overwhelmed but still functional. It looks like someone who is quiet, someone who is "in their head," someone who is just going through a phase.

But from the other side, withdrawal feels like abandonment in slow motion. Short replies can feel like dismissal. Lack of curiosity can feel like indifference. Emotional absence can feel like rejection. The person you love begins to feel alone while sitting right next to you. And they don't always know what to call it. They just know something is missing.

Presence.

What makes it more confusing is that the mask still works in public.

In public, I could still perform. I could still laugh. I could still charm. I could still be engaging. I could still appear warm, alive, connected. People saw energy and ease. They saw someone who was "fine."

That contrast can be devastating privately. Because the person closest to you sees something else: absence. Distance. Disinterest. Emotional vacancy. And they wonder what's wrong with them that you can be present for strangers but not for them.

The answer isn't that strangers matter more.

The answer is that the mask was built for performance, not intimacy.

Performance has rules. It has scripts. It has control. It has an exit. Intimacy has none of that. Intimacy requires staying when you want to run. It requires being seen when you want to hide. It requires telling the truth when silence feels safer.

The mask is excellent at short bursts. It is excellent at superficial connection. It is excellent at being admired. It is not built for sustained closeness.

And the cost of wearing it is exhaustion.

Inside, I felt tired in a way sleep couldn't fix. Numb in a way distraction couldn't solve. Hollow in a way achievements couldn't fill. The laughter didn't reach all the way in. The social ease didn't translate to emotional presence.

So at home, I had less to give.

And instead of naming that—naming my grief, my fear, my depression, my internal collapse—I went quiet. I disappeared in plain sight.

When internal emptiness grows, people look for relief. They look for something that makes them feel alive for a moment. Something that cuts through the fog. Something that quiets the ache.

And relief is seductive because it works quickly.

For me, relief often came through distraction and validation. Through small escapes. Through attention that felt regulating because it required less vulnerability than true intimacy. It offered a brief sense of being seen without requiring the terrifying act of being fully known.

But attention given elsewhere is attention not given where it matters most.

And the quiet ways distance hurts are cumulative. They stack. They compound. They become proof to the other person that they are alone. That they are not chosen. That their needs are inconvenient. That they are asking for too much.

Love can exist inside a person who is still unavailable.

That is one of the most painful truths I've ever had to accept.

I loved deeply, and still I could not meet the emotional needs of the person I loved. Not because I didn't care, but because I didn't know how to stay present without hiding. Love alone was not enough. Intention alone was not enough.

Capacity mattered.

And the shame of that contradiction is heavy. The shame of knowing you care and still causing pain. The shame of watching someone you love reach for you while you retreat.

That shame can fuel more withdrawal. It can make honesty feel unbearable. It can make repair feel impossible. It can create a cycle where you hide because you're ashamed, and you're ashamed because you're hiding.

Eventually, the most honest thing you can do is name what was missing.

Not love.

Presence.

Emotional availability. Communication. The ability to stay when discomfort rises. The willingness to ask for help instead of disappearing. The capacity to tell the truth about what is happening inside you.

These are skills. And if they were never modeled, never taught, never practiced in safety, they don't magically appear because you love someone.

They must be learned.

Naming these patterns is not an attempt to escape responsibility.

It is an attempt to understand responsibility accurately. I take responsibility for withdrawing. I take responsibility for not showing up emotionally. I take responsibility for seeking relief in ways that created distance.

I take responsibility for the impact.

And at the same time, I can acknowledge the internal forces that made those choices feel like survival.

Both truths exist. Understanding is not absolution. It is the foundation of change.

Chapter 18

Learning to Stay Present Instead of Escaping

Staying present sounds simple until you try to do it when your body is screaming to leave.

For someone shaped by trauma, presence is not neutral. Presence is exposure. Presence is risk. Presence is contact with everything you once learned to hide: fear, longing, shame, uncertainty, need.

Escaping is easier. Escaping is quick.. Escaping Works. For a moment, it lowers the pressure. It dulls the ache. It quiets the internal alarm. It restores the illusion of control.

So learning to stay present is not about motivation or willpower. It is about retraining a nervous system that learned, long ago, that disappearance was safer than staying.

Escape rarely looks dramatic. It doesn't always look like running away. More often, it looks like subtle vanishing. You're there, but you're not there. You're listening, but you're not hearing.

You're responding, but you're not connected.

You're scrolling. You're busy. You're distracted. You're doing anything that creates distance between you and the moment you are in.

And what makes it hard is that escape can feel like relief. It can feel like self-care. It can feel like peace. Especially when your internal world is loud.

But escape is not peace.
It is avoidance.
And avoidance has consequences.

Presence requires contact with inner experience, and inner experience can be brutal when it has been ignored for years. Presence means feeling the ache without immediately numbing it. It means sitting in uncertainty without demanding a quick answer. It means allowing discomfort to exist without treating it like an emergency. The body often leaves before the mind does. The first signs of escape are not decisions, they are sensations. Restlessness. Tightness. Fog. A pull toward distraction. A sudden impatience. A desire to end the conversation. A feeling of being trapped.

This is where change begins: not in forcing yourself to "be better," but in noticing the moment before you disappear.

At first, awareness comes late. You realize you checked out after the fact. That's not failure. That's the beginning of the pathway. Recognition builds the muscle.

Over time, you notice earlier. The urge to deflect. The urge to pick up your phone. The urge to turn the conversation into a joke. The urge to retreat into silence.

And in that small space, something new becomes possible. Choice.

Not a big dramatic choice. A small one. A breath.
A pause.

A sentence.

This is hard for me right now. I'm getting overwhelmed. I want to stay, but I feel myself pulling away.

These sentences are terrifying for someone who learned early that vulnerability gets punished. But they are also a form of rescue. They rescue the moment from becoming distance. They bring honesty into the room before escape takes over.

Presence is not endurance. It is regulation. It is learning how to stay without flooding. How to remain connected without collapsing. How to hold discomfort without turning it into destruction.

Presence requires safety.

Not perfection.

Not being fixed.

Safety grows through consistency. Through therapy, through grounded relationships, through self-compassion, through learning emotional language. Through practices that teach the body that the present is not the past.

Staying present is uncomfortable at first because it exposes what was buried. The sadness you avoided. The fear you outran. The longing you numbed. The shame you hid behind competence.

When you stop escaping, you start feeling.

And feeling can be terrifying when you've spent a lifetime surviving.

But slowly, presence becomes less threatening. The nervous system begins to learn that discomfort does not equal danger. That silence does not mean abandonment. That vulnerability does not automatically lead to harm.

Each time you stay, even briefly, you strengthen a new pathway.

Each time you choose honesty over disappearance, you weaken the old reflex.
Staying is a quiet form of courage. It is not dramatic. It

will not be applauded. It will not always feel like progress.

But it is the work.

This is a new definition of strength. Strength is staying when you want to run.
Strength is speaking when silence feels safer. Strength is tolerating discomfort without escaping. Strength is choosing presence even when fear is loud.

And this is how a life begins to change—not through one grand transformation, but through a thousand small moments where you stay.

Chapter 19

The Loss That Changed Everything

Some losses don't simply hurt. They dismantle you. They reach past emotion and rewire your nervous system, tear through the scaffolding of your identity, and rearrange the way time moves inside your body. They do not arrive as moments you endure and survive. They arrive as forces slow at first, almost polite, then relentless, consuming, taking what they want piece by piece until you are left standing in the aftermath trying to remember the shape of the life you used to live inside.

This loss did not come all at once. It came gradually, deceptively, wearing the disguise of ordinary strain. It began as tension I tried to rationalize, as fatigue I told myself would pass, as distance I believed could be bridged later. It arrived in pauses between conversations, in words left unsaid, in the quiet spaces where connection used to live. At first, nothing felt catastrophic. It felt manageable. Fixable. Temporary. But it kept advancing. It hardened. It widened. It learned how to live between us. And by the time I realized what it was becoming, it had already learned how to survive without resistance.

When it finally broke, it didn't break like a single event. It fractured everything at once.
I didn't just lose a marriage. I lost an entire world that

had wrapped itself around me slowly, lovingly, until it felt permanent. I lost a family that had become my family. I lost the comfort of knowing where I belonged on ordinary days. I lost traditions that weren't technically mine but had been gifted to me through shared time and shared meaning. I lost the ease of walking into a familiar space and feeling held by it without effort. I lost names I had grown used to speaking as if they would always have a place in my future. I lost birthdays, holidays, inside jokes, casual check-ins, routines that once felt mundane and now feel irreplaceable. I lost the architecture of belonging itself.

Aside from losing one of my closest friends earlier that year, nothing has ever cut me open like this.

Because this loss didn't feel like the end of a chapter. It felt like erasure. Like being removed from a life I had built my sense of self around. Like waking up and realizing the room still exists, the furniture still stands, the walls still remember but your place in it has been emptied. It felt like the world continued forward at a normal pace while something inside me refused to accept the rewrite. Every day felt split between what was real and what my body still expected to find.

And then came the most brutal part. The part grief doesn't prepare you for. The part no one wants to talk about.

This wasn't only something that happened to me. It was something I participated in.

Not because love was missing. It wasn't. Not because care was absent. It never was. But love and care are not the same as capacity. And capacity is not the same as intention. I had been living on survival wiring for so long that fear often drove without announcing itself.

My nervous system chose protection over presence. Control over openness. Retreat over honesty. I didn't always recognize it while it was happening. Sometimes I only saw it after the impact—after the moment had passed, after the damage had already settled into the space between us.

That realization changes grief. It deepens it. It sharpens it. It contaminates it with shame.

Because now you are not only mourning what you lost. You are mourning the version of yourself who didn't yet know how to stop the unraveling. You are grieving not just the relationship, but the moments you mishandled while believing you were doing the best you could.

You are forced to sit with the knowledge that intention does not cancel impact, and love does not automatically override patterns forged in fear.

And once that door opens, the mind turns cruel. You replay everything.

The conversations you rushed through instead of staying present. The moments you withdrew when honesty felt too exposing.

The times you numbed yourself instead of sitting inside discomfort.

The exits you took small, quiet exits because they felt safer than staying emotionally visible. The promises you made to yourself to show up differently and then broke without meaning to.

Regret does not visit gently. It hunts. It stalks the quiet moments. It waits for stillness. It crawls into your bed at night and sits on your chest. It meets you in mirrors and reflections. It hijacks memory and weaponizes it. Songs become traps. Places become evidence. Even joy feels suspicious, as if happiness itself is a betrayal of what was lost.

And the phone becomes its own form of torture.

Every vibration ignites hope.
Every notification feels loaded with possibility. Every silence becomes confirmation of distance.

Days stretch. Hours drag. The absence of contact becomes louder than any argument ever was. The mind starts negotiating with time, with memory, with reality itself. Maybe tomorrow. Maybe after space. Maybe when emotions cool. Maybe when something shifts.
And beneath all of that, the real questions wait. Will you reach back?

Will something soften?

Will I ever be seen again the way I was seen there?

And then the darker questions arrive, uninvited and merciless. What if nothing changes?

What if this is permanent?

What if I must live the rest of my life carrying this awareness?

That is where grief mutates. It stops being about sadness and becomes a daily confrontation with irreversibility. It becomes waking up every morning and remembering again that the future you were building no longer exists.

It becomes understanding something intellectually while your body refuses to comply. It becomes learning that acceptance is not a single moment, but a thousand small surrenders you are forced into one by one.

And because I was already shaped by old trauma, this loss didn't just hurt. It detonated beliefs that had been waiting quietly beneath the surface.
Connection leads to danger. Closeness ends in pain.
Attachment equals loss.
Hope is followed by devastation.

So even while I was desperate for reconnection, my body was trying to shield me from it. Longing and fear collided constantly. One part of me reached forward. Another part braced for impact. I lived suspended between desire and defense, between wanting closeness and preparing for harm, until I could no longer tell which reactions were present and which were echoes.

The tragedy is not that love was absent. The tragedy is that love alone was not enough to override survival. Love did not automatically rewire a nervous system trained to anticipate loss. Love did not erase patterns built to keep me safe when safety once depended on distance. Love did not cure fear—it exposed it.

And when everything finally settled into reality, when the noise faded and the consequences remained, the truth left behind was devastatingly simple.

I lost a world.

And I had to live inside the awareness that some of the force that destroyed it came from within me.

That knowledge changes a person. It strips away illusions. It leaves no room for easy narratives. It either collapses you into self-hatred, or it drives you toward the only thing that still resembles dignity.

Not punishment. Not grand gestures. Not performance. Responsibility. Responsibility to see clearly.

Responsibility to stop running from discomfort.

Responsibility to understand the damage without minimizing it or drowning in it.

Responsibility to become someone who no longer let's fear dictate connection.

That is where this loss leads. Not to forgetting. Not to erasing love. But to reckoning. And that reckoning—slow, painful, unavoidable—is where the next chapter begins.

Chapter 20

There comes a point where explanations stop soothing you.

You can understand your childhood. You can name the patterns. You can trace the wiring from the origin point to the present day. You can map your fear, your avoidance, your shame, your reflexes. You can recognize the moment you start to withdraw, the moment you start to numb out, the moment you start to reach for anything that reduces discomfort quickly.

And still the consequences remain. The loss stays.

The silence stays. The distance stays.

The door stays closed.

This is where people either collapse or change.

Because consequences carry a particular kind of psychological pressure: they tempt you to treat pain as proof. Proof that you care. Proof that you've paid. Proof that you're not the villain. Proof that you're "good" because you're suffering.

But suffering is not accountability. Suffering is not growth. Suffering is just suffering—and if you build your identity around it, you end up chained to the worst moment of your life as if it's the only thing true about you.

The mind wants punishment because punishment feels like control. If I can punish myself enough, maybe the universe will reverse it. If I can suffer deeply enough, maybe I'll deserve repair. If I can hurt myself hard enough, maybe I won't have to face the unbearable truth: some things don't come back.

But life doesn't operate like that.

Consequences are not cosmic sentences. They are outcomes. They are reality following action. They don't ask whether you meant harm or whether you're sorry. They simply exist.

And the hardest part is irreversibility.

There are consequences you can repair with effort. There are consequences you can soften with time.

And there are consequences that remain permanent no matter how much you grow. That truth is where hope gets tested.

Because there is a kind of hope that is just denial wearing optimism. That hope says, "This will go back. This will reset. This will return to what it was."

When you cling to that hope, you keep living in the past, bargaining with a reality that doesn't bargain back.
Real hope is different.

Real hope is not the belief that everything will be restored. Real hope is the decision not to become your worst outcome.

Real hope says:

> *I will live with integrity even if I never get the ending I wanted.*
> *I will learn even if learning comes too late to save what I lost.*
> *I will change even if no one watches.*
> *I will stop running even if staying hurts.*

That kind of hope doesn't feel like light. It feels like resolve. It feels like waking up and choosing the difficult thing again. It feels like resisting the urge to disappear into shame. It feels like holding the truth without collapsing into it.

Because shame wants a simple story. Shame wants a label. Shame wants a verdict. You're bad.

You ruin things.
You don't deserve love. This is who you are.

But consequences do not define identity unless you surrender to them. Responsibility is different than shame.

Shame says: I am irredeemable.

Responsibility says: I did harm and I am capable of change.

Responsibility does not ask for self-destruction as proof. It asks for honesty. It asks for restraint. It asks for action aligned with values, not with fear.

It asks you to stop performing remorse and start living differently.

That is where the real fight begins—not against the past, but against the reflex to escape the pain of the present.

Because living with consequences means you don't get to numb out and call it survival anymore. It means you don't get to hide and call it protection anymore. It means you don't get to punish yourself and call it accountability anymore.

It means you have to build a life that can hold what happened without being defined by it. And that is harder than grief, because grief is a storm.

Building is daily.

Building is waking up and choosing steadiness when your mind wants chaos. Building is staying present when your body screams for escape. Building is learning to tolerate the ache without trying to erase it through distraction, validation, or disappearance.

This is where hope becomes practical. Not hope as a fantasy.

Hope as a discipline. And discipline, in its healthiest form, is not domination. It is commitment.

Commitment to truth.
Commitment to change.
Commitment to not repeating the same damage in different clothing.

The question is no longer: how I undo this.

The question becomes: how do I live now.

Chapter 21

The People Who Stayed, and the Work That Began

There is a particular kind of grace in the people who stay. Not the ones who offer slogans. Not the ones who try to fix you like a problem. Not the ones who get uncomfortable and disappear the moment your pain stops being entertaining or simple.

The ones who stay do something else. They listen.
They answer the phone even when your voice sounds the same as it did yesterday. They let you circle back again and again to the same grief, because grief is not linear, and trauma does not resolve neatly. They tolerate repetition. They tolerate mess. They tolerate the silence in the middle of your sentences when you can't find language for something too heavy to carry cleanly.

They don't flinch.

And for someone shaped by abandonment, that steadiness is destabilizing at first. You don't trust it. You wait for the impatience. You wait for the moment your sadness becomes a burden. You wait for the withdrawal, because you learned early that people leave when you need too much.

So when someone stays, your nervous system doesn't immediately relax. It goes on high alert. Is this real? How long will it last? When will they turn away?

This is one of the crueler injuries trauma leaves behind: even care can trigger fear.

But slowly, something begins to shift—not in the mind, but in the body. The expectation of abandonment weakens, not because someone convinced you with words, but because they proved it with presence.

And that presence becomes scaffolding. Not a solution. Scaffolding. Because support holds you, but it cannot rebuild you.

That's where the work begins.

The work is not glamorous. It doesn't come with applause. It doesn't arrive like a dramatic transformation. It arrives as repetition. It arrives as routine. It arrives as choosing not to disappear in the moments you most want to.

The work began when I stopped asking, "How do I get my life back," and started asking, "How do I stop living like I'm still in danger?"

Because the truth is, danger had shaped my entire

nervous system. It had taught me to respond, to react, to protect, to anticipate, to control. It had taught me to manage emotion like a bomb technician—carefully, quickly, always expecting something to explode.
But healing required something different.

It required learning to stay in discomfort without turning it into a crisis. It required learning to regulate without escape. It required learning to feel without drowning.
It required rebuilding capacity.

Mental capacity to reflect instead of react.

Emotional capacity to tolerate uncertainty without grabbing for control. Relational capacity to communicate fear instead of masking it as distance.
Physical capacity to move stress through the body instead of storing it like a silent disease. This work looked like small decisions that didn't feel heroic.
It looked like getting up when shame wanted me to stay down. It looked like moving my body when grief wanted to freeze it. It looked like choosing structure when chaos felt familiar.

It looked like telling the truth when silence felt safer.
And the people who stayed—friends who listened, friends who held the line, friends who didn't abandon me in my worst season—became the mirrors that helped me see myself clearly without condemning me.

That is a rare gift.

Because condemnation shuts you down. Compassion keeps you open.

And open is where change happens.

Chapter 22

Rebuilding Identity After Collapse

Collapse doesn't just knock the wind out of you. It takes your name. It strips you down until the versions of yourself you used to rely on can't even stand up anymore. It exposes what you were using to survive and forces one brutal question you can't distract yourself from:

Who am I when I'm not performing?

For most of my life, identity wasn't something I discovered. It was something I constructed under pressure. A structure built to hold back panic, built to keep me functional, built to keep me moving even when I was bleeding internally. It looked like confidence. It looked like control. It looked like charm. It looked like intensity. It looked like competence.

It looked like strength.

But collapse has no respect for appearances. Collapse doesn't negotiate. It doesn't care what people think you are. Collapse shows you exactly what was real and what was armor.

When everything finally broke, I didn't just lose a relationship. I lost the self I used to navigate the world. The mask I wore so long it stopped feeling like a mask. The role I played so consistently it started to feel like personality. And without it, there was a frightening emptiness— like stepping into a room where the lights are off and realizing you don't know where anything is. The old identity was built on roles. The one who holds it together.

The one who doesn't need anyone. The one who stays composed.

The one who fixes. The one who performs.

Those roles were not vanity. They were survival. They were the structure that kept me from falling apart when I didn't have language for what was happening inside me. They were the way I stayed upright when no one else was holding me.

But when those roles collapsed, it felt like losing myself.

And the truth was worse than that.
It felt like meeting myself.

Because beneath performance, there was grief. Beneath control, there was fear. Beneath intensity, there was a nervous system trained to brace. Beneath charm, there was longing—raw and exposed—trying to be seen without being punished for needing.

This is the part no one prepares you for: after collapse, you don't immediately rebuild into something confident. You drift. You question everything. You stand in the ruins and realize you don't know what you like, what you need, what you actually believe—because you were so busy surviving that you never got to find out.

The hardest nights were the ones with no distraction. The ones where silence wasn't peaceful—it was loud. It dragged every unresolved feeling into the room and forced me to sit with it. It forced me to face the ache I had been outrunning for years.

And once you see the truth, you can't unsee it. You see how fear shaped your habits.

You see how shame shaped your choices.
You see how protection shaped your personality.
You see how survival became identity so gradually you never noticed it happening. Hypervigilance became "awareness."

Control became "responsibility."
Emotional distance became "strength."
Self-reliance became "independence."

And because those traits are praised, no one asks what they cost. Collapse shows you the cost.

It shows you that being "the strong one" can be a way of refusing to need. It shows you that being "the independent one" can be a way of never risking disappointment. It shows you that being "in control" can be a way of keeping love at arm's length so it can't hurt you.

But the cost of those strategies is intimacy.

Because the version of you built for survival can function. It can succeed. It can impress. But it cannot always connect.

So rebuilding identity wasn't about becoming someone new. It was about recovering what had been buried under fear. It was about pulling the real self out from under years of bracing.

And that didn't happen with declarations. It happened with small actions.

The Quiet That Raised Me

It happened when I chose to stay present instead of checking out. When I told the truth instead of managing perception.

When I paused instead of reacting.

When I stopped turning every emotion into a problem to solve and started letting it be information.

Identity stopped being something I claimed and became something I practiced. Because after collapse, you don't rebuild with confidence.

You rebuild with honesty.

And honesty is the first thing that ever felt like real safety.

Chapter 23

Learning to Love Without Losing Yourself

For most of my life, love did not feel like a place to rest. It felt like a test I had to pass. It felt like something I had to **earn**, something I had to *manage*, something I had to *keep from breaking*. I did not enter relationships assuming safety. I entered them scanning for consequences. I entered them bracing for the moment closeness would turn into a demand, or a disappointment, or a withdrawal that left me standing alone with my own need.

I didn't understand that I was bringing my childhood into every room I loved in. I didn't understand that my nervous system was still negotiating the terms of attachment like it was negotiating survival. I thought I was being careful. I thought I was being mature. I thought I was being strong. But what I was really doing was protecting myself in ways that looked like love from the outside and felt like fear from the inside.

When love is learned in unsafe environments, it never feels simple. It becomes conditional by default. You learn to attach with one hand while keeping the other hand on the door. You learn to *give* while staying ready to *lose.* You learn to read mood, track tone, anticipate disappointment, and adjust yourself before the other person even asks. You learn that being "easy to love" is safer than being real. You learn to keep the parts of you that feel messy, needy, tender, or uncertain out of view, because in your body, those parts still feel like liabilities. And then you grow up and think you're free.

But the first time you love someone for real, the old learning wakes up.

Because intimacy doesn't just bring closeness. It brings exposure. It brings emotional weight. It brings moments where you can't rely on charm, or competence, or control. It brings the kind of presence you can't fake for long. It asks you to show up as yourself, not as your mask.

That's where I started to lose myself.

Not all at once. Not dramatically. Quietly.

I lost myself in the small choices that looked harmless. I lost myself every time I swallowed a feeling to avoid conflict. Every time I softened the truth so I wouldn't be "too much."

Every time I said "it's fine" while my body was tightening and my chest was burning with something I couldn't name. Every time I pretended, I didn't need reassurance because needing anything still felt like a risk.

At first, it felt like love. It felt like sacrifice. It felt like loyalty. But over time, it became erasure.

Because when you consistently override your own experience to keep connection, you don't become safer. You become smaller. You become quieter. You become less visible in your own relationship. You start living as an edited version of yourself, hoping the relationship will hold, while privately grieving the fact that you can't relax inside it.

And that is one of the cruelest paradoxes of trauma: you can crave intimacy and still fear the very things intimacy requires. You can want closeness and still flinch at dependency. You can love someone and still struggle to let them fully have you.

The fear is not always obvious. It doesn't always look like panic. Sometimes it looks like competence. Sometimes it looks like control. Sometimes it looks like emotional containment that gets praised as "strength." Sometimes it looks like silence.

It looks like staying calm, but not staying open.

It looks like being present, but not being reachable. It looks like love with the volume turned down.

And the person you love feels it. They feel the distance. They feel the hesitation. They feel the way your body stays guarded even when your words say you care. They feel the gap between affection and availability. They feel how often your attention drifts when the moment requires you to stay.

And if you have any conscience at all, you feel it too. You feel the contradiction. You feel the shame of being loved and still holding back. You feel the pressure of someone's needs meeting your fear. You feel yourself tightening, withdrawing, managing, controlling, escaping—anything but staying raw and honest in the exact moment honesty is needed.

That's when love starts to feel like a threat.

Not because the person is unsafe, but because the nervous system is still living by older rules. Rules that say closeness precedes pain. Rules that say if you show your need, you will be punished, rejected, mocked, or abandoned. Rules that say you have to stay in control to stay safe.

So you start performing again.

You become helpful instead of vulnerable. You become competent instead of honest. You become charming instead of present. You become agreeable instead of real. You start offering what you can give—solutions, effort, gifts, plans—while avoiding what intimacy asks for: access to your inner world.

Because access still feels like exposure.

This is where I had to face something painful: love without selfhood is not intimacy. It's endurance. It's survival wearing romance. It's the old mask pretending it's a relationship.

Learning to love without losing myself meant learning to do the opposite of what my instincts demanded. It meant learning to stop disappearing in the moments I felt threatened. It meant learning to **name** what was happening inside me before it turned into withdrawal or control. It meant learning to say the words that felt humiliating at first, the ones that made me feel small, the ones that triggered the old shame:

I'm overwhelmed.
I'm scared.
I feel myself shutting down.
I need reassurance.
I don't know how to stay present right now, but I want to try.

Those sentences are not impressive. They don't make you look powerful. They don't give you the upper hand. They don't let you hide behind competence.

They do something better. They create truth.
And truth is the only thing love can stand on.

I also had to learn that boundaries aren't abandonment. Boundaries aren't walls. Boundaries aren't rejection. Boundaries are structure. They are the frame that keeps love from collapsing under weight it was never meant to carry.

A boundary says: I'm here, and I'm real.
A boundary says: I want connection, but I won't erase myself to keep it.
A boundary says: I can stay without surrendering my whole identity.

For someone like me, that was a revolution.

Because the child in me believed love required self-erasure. The child in me believed safety came from compliance. The child in me believed the price of being kept was being small. The adult in me had to unlearn that. The adult in me had to decide that love would no longer be something I survived.

It would be something I participated in.

Learning to love without losing myself was not a single decision. It was a series of moments where I chose presence over performance. Honesty over management. Vulnerability over control. It was slow. It was imperfect. It was uncomfortable in ways I wasn't prepared for.

But it was real.

And real was the only kind of love I ever actually wanted.

Chapter 24

When Healing Ebbs and Flows and People Fall Away

Healing doesn't happen like a victory. It happens like weather. It moves in patterns you can't control and doesn't care what day you hoped to have. Some mornings you wake up and feel steady, like the ground is finally under you. Other mornings you wake up and feel the same ache you thought you outgrew pressing into your chest like it never left.

That swing can make you doubt everything. It can make you believe you're failing. It can make you question whether all the work matters if the pain still returns.

But healing was never a straight line. It was never meant to be.

Healing advances, retreats, pauses, resurfaces. It rewinds you into old feelings with new awareness. It forces you to face the same wound from different angles until the nervous system finally learns what the mind has tried to believe: that pain is not the same as danger, and emotion is not the same as collapse.

The hardest part was learning to stay steady when the process wasn't.

Because when you start healing, you stop running the old programs. You stop numbing the way you used to numb. You stop distracting yourself the way you used to distract. You stop performing strength when you're breaking. You start slowing down. You start telling the truth. You start speaking in a voice that isn't trying to impress anyone.

You become less entertaining. Less shiny. Less convenient. You become real.

And real rearranges your life.

Not everyone knows what to do with the real you.

Some people loved the version of you that never asked for too much. Some people were comfortable with the version of you that was always strong, always funny, always "fine." Some people built their relationship with you around your role—your usefulness, your energy, your ability to keep things light, your willingness to carry your pain quietly.

When you start healing, that version of you begins to fade. And that is when people begin to drift.

It rarely happens loudly. It rarely arrives with a confrontation. It happens in silence. It happens in timing. It happens in distance that grows a little at a time until the absence is undeniable.

Texts that used to come quickly start arriving late, then not at all. Invitations stop. Calls go unanswered. The connection that once felt automatic starts feeling like effort, and you're the only one still trying to hold it.

At first, you make excuses for it. You assume they're busy. You tell yourself you're being sensitive. You try to act normal. You try to be easy again.

Because the old survival system wakes up and starts negotiating:

If I become lighter, they'll come back. If I stop talking about it, they'll stay.
If I perform strength again, I'll be safe.

And for a person shaped by abandonment, nothing is more tempting than shrinking yourself to avoid being left.

But healing doesn't let you live there anymore.

Because once you start seeing your patterns, you can't unsee them. Once you start reclaiming your voice, you can't go back to silence without feeling the cost. Once you start telling the truth, performance starts to feel like betrayal of yourself.

So you have to sit with the hardest possibility:

Some people will not stay for the version of you that is healing.

That truth can feel like a second trauma. It can feel like proof that the old fear was right—that honesty drives people away, that need is dangerous, that vulnerability costs you connection.

But the deeper truth is more complex.

People drift for many reasons that have nothing to do with your worth. Some people don't have the emotional capacity to sit with grief. Some people are afraid of depth because it stirs their own pain. Some people only know how to connect through distraction, and when you stop distracting, they don't know how to meet you. Some people liked the old dynamic because it was predictable, because it kept you in a role they understood.

And when you step out of that role, the relationship loses its structure. This is where the grief becomes sharp.

Because it's not just the loss of the relationship. It's the way it happens. The ambiguity. The unanswered questions. The silence that offers no closure. The slow fading that makes you feel disposable, even if that was never anyone's intention.

Ambiguous loss has a particular cruelty: it leaves you holding the ending alone.

And if you carry old abandonment wounds, that loneliness doesn't stay in the present. It reaches backward and grabs every earlier moment you were left, every earlier moment you were ignored, every earlier moment you learned not to need anyone because needing meant pain.

So the nervous system reacts.

You overthink.
You replay conversations.
You scan for what you did wrong.
You blame yourself automatically because that was always the safest story.
You start preparing to be alone, because that preparation feels like control.

And then healing asks you to do something almost impossible:

Do not chase what is leaving.
Do not beg for closeness from people who cannot offer it.
Do not punish yourself for someone else's distance.
Do not return to the mask just to keep a seat at a table that no longer fits you.

That restraint is agony at first. It feels like sitting still while something important walks away. It feels like swallowing your own panic. It feels like choosing dignity when your body wants to sprint after attachment.

But it is also power.

Because for the first time, you are not abandoning yourself to avoid being abandoned by someone else.
And that becomes the suspense inside healing: not whether people stay, but whether you stay with yourself when they don't.

Because there are two kinds of loneliness.

The loneliness of being alone.
And the loneliness of being with people while you're not allowed to be yourself. The second one is worse.

So you begin to choose a different loneliness—the kind that has integrity in it, the kind that has room for truth, the kind that isn't built on performance. You start letting the drift happen without turning it into a verdict on your identity. You start allowing endings without begging for explanations you may never get.

And slowly, something changes.

You stop chasing.
You stop bargaining.
You stop shrinking.
You start building a life that can hold your real emotional weight.

And then, quietly, new connections begin to form—not fast, not flashy, not dramatic. They form slowly, like trust forms. They form around shared values rather than shared distraction. They form with people who don't require you to perform to be accepted. They don't rush your healing. They don't demand a lighter version of you. They don't punish your truth. They don't disappear when you're human.

Those relationships feel different. They feel steadier. They feel calmer. They feel like something your nervous system can rest inside of, even if only for a moment at first.

Healing is tidal. It comes and goes. It rises and recedes. And yes, sometimes people fall away in the shifting. But what matters most is what you build in the quiet space that remains.

Because the real work of healing is not proving you are lovable. It is finally acting like you believe it.

Chapter 25

Why You Can't Heal by Jumping Into Another Relationship

After a relationship ends—especially the kind that takes pieces of you with it—the silence doesn't just settle. It presses. It pounds. It fills the rooms you used to share with plans and laughter and routine, and it makes everything you do feel louder than it should. Your phone feels heavier in your hand. Your bed feels too large. Your evenings stretch out like empty highways with no exits. And in that quiet, something desperate starts whispering a familiar promise:

Find someone new. Fill this.

Prove you're still wanted. Prove you're still chosen. Make the ache stop.

When loss hits, the nervous system does not calmly request healing. It demands relief. It craves contact like oxygen. It searches for a body, a voice, a message, a touch—anything that will interrupt the feeling that you've been left behind in your own life. If you've spent a lifetime equating connection with safety, that craving doesn't feel optional. It feels like survival.

It feels like an emergency.

And that's what makes the temptation so dangerous. Because you can absolutely replace a person. But you cannot replace the work.

You cannot outsource grief. You cannot delegate accountability. You cannot hand your emptiness to a stranger and ask them to return you to yourself. You can climb into another relationship and still bring the same unhealed nervous system with you—still carrying the same fear, the same shame, the same patterns waiting beneath your skin like a storm that never finished forming.

At first, a new connection can feel like a rescue. It can feel like blood returning to a numb limb. Someone texts you back quickly. Someone laughs at your jokes. Someone looks at you like you're still worth something. Your body lights up. Your mind speeds up. Your appetite returns. You start sleeping again. You start believing you're okay.

But what's happening isn't healing. It's stimulation.

It's the nervous system trading depth for dopamine. It's the heart trading integration for intensity. It's the pain getting covered, not cleared.

The wound gets dressed up in new attention, and for a moment, it looks like it disappeared.

But a covered wound still bleeds.

New romance can flood you with temporary relief the way a shot of adrenaline floods the body with temporary power. You feel alive again, and aliveness feels like progress. It feels like proof that you're recovering. It feels like the story is turning in your favor.
But relief is not repair.

Relief is a pause in the pain, not a transformation of it.

And when you use a relationship as relief, you quietly assign it a job it cannot survive.
Because somewhere underneath the flirting and the chemistry and the late-night conversations, the new person becomes more than a person. They become a stabilizer. A regulator. A mirror you need to hold still so you can recognize yourself again. They become the one who is supposed to keep you from collapsing, the one who is supposed to quiet your shame, the one who is supposed to make you feel chosen when you can't choose yourself.

They become a bandage for a wound they didn't create.
And bandages eventually come off.
When grief and shame haven't been metabolized, the

new relationship starts carrying invisible demands. Not spoken, not admitted, sometimes not even understood by the person making them.

It begins silently:

Stay close so I don't feel abandoned.

Reassure me so I don't have to sit with my self-hatred.

Want me so I don't have to face my emptiness.
Love me loudly so I don't hear my regret.

The relationship becomes less about two people meeting and more about one person trying to outrun themselves. This is how "moving on" becomes avoidance with a heartbeat.

Because what you don't process doesn't disappear. It waits. It follows. It collects interest.

You can change the face across the table, but you can't change the patterns inside your body by swapping out the person who triggers them. Without internal work, the same structure reappears. The same fear rises. The same defenses activate. The same exits get built. The same urgency shows up the moment the honeymoon phase stops drowning out your nervous system's deeper alarms.

At some point, the new person disappoints you—not because they're cruel, but because they're human. They don't text back fast enough. They get quiet. They have a bad day. They need space. They disagree with you. They don't respond the way your nervous system demands.

And suddenly you feel it: that old familiar drop in your stomach, that internal freefall, that primal terror that whispers, Here it is again.

This is why the pattern repeats.

Because when the internal system is still organized around threat, love becomes something you chase, test, manage, or control. You lean too hard. You pull away too fast. You overexplain. You overthink. You read tone like it's a weapon. You confuse uncertainty with danger. You become hyperaware of the tiniest shifts, and your body reacts like the relationship is a battlefield.

The faces change, but the nervous system doesn't. And then the shame returns with teeth.

Because deep down you know you're not just dating someone—you're using the relationship to escape what you refuse to sit with. You may not say it out loud. You may not mean it cruelly.

But the truth still presses:

If being alone feels unbearable, it's because you haven't learned how to stay with yourself. That sentence hits hard because it exposes the real work.

Healing is slow. Healing is quiet. Healing doesn't offer fireworks. Healing asks you to do the one thing trauma trained you not to do: *stay.*

Stay when the loneliness tightens around your ribs. Stay when your mind starts bargaining.

Stay when your body wants to run toward anyone who will hold you. Stay when the old wound says, If you're alone, you're unsafe.

Because this is the myth that breaks people: that being alone is the same as being unloved.

Trauma makes solitude feel like danger because solitude once meant no protection. It meant no witness. It meant no rescue. So the body panics when it's left alone with emotion. It starts searching for a way out—any way out.

A new relationship is a tempting exit.

It looks like warmth. It looks like movement. It looks like a new story.
But if you climb into it too quickly, you aren't starting a new story—you're dragging the old one into a new room and hoping the lighting will hide it.
The most difficult and transformative thing you can do after loss is not to "move on." It's to
move inward.

The Quiet That Raised Me

To sit in the quiet without trying to fill it with someone else's attention. To let the grief rise without drowning it in flirting.

To let the regret speak without silencing it with validation.

To let the shame show itself without rushing to be desired as proof you're still worthy.

That kind of solitude isn't isolation. It's integration.

It is learning to be with your own emotions without abandoning yourself. It is learning to tolerate your own company without treating it like punishment. It is rebuilding self-trust—slowly, deliberately—until your nervous system begins to understand that you can feel pain without being destroyed by it.

This is where readiness is forged.

Readiness isn't the absence of longing. Readiness isn't pretending you don't want love. Readiness is when love stops being a rescue mission and becomes a choice.

There's a difference between wanting connection and needing it to save you.

If what you're really asking a new relationship to do is make you whole, you aren't ready. If you're asking it to erase your grief, you aren't ready. If you're asking it to silence your shame, you aren't ready. If you're asking it to prove you're not broken, you aren't ready.

Because wholeness can't be handed to you. It has to be built.

And the building is not glamorous. It's repetitive. It's private. It's the daily work of turning toward your internal world instead of sprinting away from it. It's learning how to regulate without running. It's learning how to breathe through discomfort. It's learning how to name what's happening inside you before it turns into action you regret.

It's creating structure where chaos used to rule.

It's developing an internal relationship strong enough to stand on its own—one built on truth instead of performance, compassion instead of punishment, accountability instead of collapse.

Because if you can't stay with yourself, you will always ask someone else to do it for you. And that is not love. That is dependence disguised as romance.

Choosing not to jump into another relationship can feel brutal at first. It can feel like refusing water when you're thirsty. It can feel like sitting in an empty room and telling your nervous system, no, we're not running this time. It can feel like holding your own shaking hands while the old survival part begs for an exit.

But that refusal is not deprivation. It is integrity.

It is you saying: I will not repeat harm just to avoid loneliness. I will not use another person to escape myself.

I will not build a connection on top of unprocessed wreckage and call it healing. Solitude, when chosen consciously, becomes preparation. It becomes the training ground for a different kind of love. A love that doesn't require urgency. A love that doesn't need to prove anything. A love that doesn't ask another person to carry your unhealed weight.

And when love comes again—and it can—it arrives differently when you've done this work. It arrives slower.

It arrives steadier.

It arrives with less panic and less desperation. It arrives without the need to be saved.

It doesn't have to rescue you to feel real. It can simply connect.

That is what healing makes possible: not the end of longing, but the end of using longing as a weapon against yourself. Not the end of love, but the end of needing love to erase your pain.

Because the truth is simple and brutal and freeing all at once:

You cannot heal through replacement. You heal through presence.

You heal through honesty.

You heal by staying long enough to meet yourself in the silence—and not running away. And the moment you can do that, you stop chasing relationships to fill a void. You start choosing connection from a place that finally feels like strength.

Chapter 26

The Silence That Tries to Recruit You

After loss, the quiet doesn't simply return—it advances. It moves into the places where love used to live and starts making itself at home. It sits at the edge of the bed, in the pause between notifications, in the empty passenger seat, in the gap between dinner and sleep.

It shows up in the seconds after you turn off the light, when your mind stops pretending it's fine and your body finally admits what it's been carrying.

Silence doesn't arrive neutral. Silence arrives with a proposal. It offers a deal in a voice you recognize: don't feel this fully, and I'll help you survive it. It doesn't say that like a threat. It says it like a promise. It says it with the confidence of something that has protected you before. And that's the problem—because part of you believes it.

The first thing the silence does is make you reach. Not always for a person, but for anything that can interrupt the rawness of being alone with yourself. You reach for your phone like it's a life raft. You reach for distraction like it's oxygen. You reach for the next conversation, the next connection, the next proof that you are still visible.

You scroll faster. You talk more. You stay busy. You keep movement in your life because stillness feels like exposure. And exposure to a nervous system trained by trauma is never just uncomfortable. It feels dangerous. It feels like standing in a room where the door doesn't lock. It feels like being seen without armor.

This is where people mistake reaction for desire. They call it "moving on," but what it often is, underneath, is the body trying to regulate panic by attaching to something new. New attention has energy. New interest has heat. New connection brings a rush that can briefly lift the weight off your chest. It can make you feel like you're back in the world again instead of watching life from behind glass. For a moment, the ache quiets. The shame loosens. The loneliness stops clawing. The nervous system exhales. And that exhale can feel like healing if you've been suffocating. But relief and healing are not the same thing. Relief is a temporary anesthesia. Healing is surgery. Relief lets you walk around with the wound covered. Healing forces you to confront what's still bleeding under the bandage.

The silence knows this. It is not naïve. It understands how quickly you will trade depth for distraction, and it pressures you with urgency that sounds like logic. It tells you that if you don't fill the void soon, you'll fall into it. It convinces you that longing is a problem that needs solving instead of an emotion that needs listening. It turns your own heart into an emergency and hands you a set of familiar tools—charm, speed, performance, intensity—like weapons you've carried for years. And because they've worked before, you pick them up automatically. You put on the mask without thinking. You smile at the right moments. You sound confident when you aren't. You become magnetic when you feel empty. You become impressive when you feel small. You turn yourself into someone who cannot be left, because being left is the thing your body never stopped fearing.

But a mask can only hold for so long before it starts demanding payment. At first, it feels like control. It feels like strength. It feels like proof that you're not broken. Yet underneath it, the truth stays awake. The truth watches the performance. The truth keeps score. And the truth knows when you are using connection as escape. That knowledge creates a tension you can't talk your way out of. It sits in your chest, in your stomach, in the way you flinch when someone asks you a simple question and you feel the urge to answer like it's a test. It sits in the way you crave reassurance but resent needing it. It sits in the way you want closeness and fear it at the same time. It sits in the contradiction that trauma builds: you hunger for love, and you mistrust it the moment it arrives.

If you jump into another relationship before you've learned how to hold yourself, you don't leave your patterns behind—you import them. You carry them into the new person's home like luggage you refuse to unpack. You bring your fear of abandonment, your reflex to withdraw, your need to control emotional weather, your instinct to earn safety through performance. At first, the new person doesn't see it because chemistry is loud and novelty is blinding. But time is honest. Time removes the glitter. Time presses on your nervous system until it reveals what it's been protecting. And eventually the old alarms return, because they were never resolved, only outrun. The moment the new person disappoints you, the moment they need space, the moment they don't respond the way your body demands, the past rushes back through the crack like smoke. You feel that drop in your stomach that doesn't match the situation. You feel that urgency to fix, to chase, to test, to punish, to vanish. You feel your mind sharpening details into danger because danger once lived in details. You feel your chest tighten as if love is about to turn into harm, because once, it did.

This is why healing cannot be outsourced. Because another person cannot rewire a nervous system that still thinks closeness is risky. Another person cannot carry your grief without eventually becoming crushed by it. Another person cannot be your proof of worth without eventually becoming your judge. When you ask a new relationship to save you from the consequences of an old life, you put a weight on intimacy that makes it collapse. And when it collapses, you don't just lose the person— you lose your temporary relief. The silence rushes back in, louder than before, and it says, see, even this didn't work. That is how people spiral. Not because they don't want to heal, but because they keep trying to heal in ways that protect them from feeling.

Real healing is the decision to stop running at the exact moment running feels necessary. It is the choice to sit in your own presence without turning it into punishment. It is learning to tolerate loneliness without interpreting it as rejection. It is learning to feel grief without demanding someone else fix it. It is learning to admit, in a voice you can live with, that you miss what you lost and that missing it doesn't mean you are weak. It means you were connected. It means you were human. It means something mattered. And the only way through that truth is through it— straight through the center—without trying to numb it with someone else's affection.

The silence will keep trying to recruit you. It will keep offering shortcuts dressed up as opportunities. It will keep whispering that the next person will solve what the last person exposed. But the work is quieter than that. The work is you learning to stay. The work is you building a self you can stand inside of, so love becomes something you choose, not something you cling to. The work is you becoming the kind of man who doesn't need a relationship to feel real, because he has learned how to be real even when no one is watching. And once you can do that, you stop chasing relief and start moving toward repair. You stop searching for someone to save you from yourself, and you start becoming someone you don't need to escape.

Chapter 27

Loneliness Without Self-Abandonment

Loneliness is not a quiet emotion. It doesn't politely wait its turn. It arrives like weather— sudden, heavy, unavoidable—and it changes the pressure inside your body before you have words for it. After loss, loneliness doesn't simply exist, it presses. It leans its full weight against

your chest in the late hours of the night. It fills the empty spaces left behind when routines dissolve and familiar voices go silent. It echoes in the rooms where life once moved easily, and it asks a single, terrifying question: what now.

When relationships end, the loss is not contained to the relationship itself. It spreads. It infiltrates the ordinary. You notice it when you wake up and there is no one to orient toward. You notice it when there is no message waiting for you, no shared plan shaping the day. You notice it in the smallest, most humiliating ways— reaching for your phone without knowing why, lingering in doorways, feeling unsure where to put your attention or your body or your breath. Loneliness does not announce itself as sadness. It announces itself as dislocation.

If your nervous system was shaped by abandonment, loneliness doesn't register as an emotion at all. It registers as threat. It wakes up the oldest fear you carry: I am alone because something is wrong with me. That belief doesn't argue politely. It asserts itself with certainty. It turns silence into accusation. It turns emptiness into evidence. It tells you that being alone means being unwanted, and being unwanted means being unsafe.

But loneliness is not a verdict. It is not a diagnosis. It is not a final judgment on your worth or your future. Loneliness is a signal—a deeply human one. It is the body's response to separation, transition, and grief. It is what arises when attachment has been disrupted and the system has not yet reorganized. The pain is not proof of deficiency. The pain is proof of capacity—capacity for connection, for attachment, for love.

The cruel irony is that loneliness often peaks not when you are failing, but when you are becoming more honest. When distractions fall away. When numbing stops working. When the old ways of escaping yourself no longer provide relief. In those moments, the quiet grows louder, and the feelings you've outrun for years finally catch up. That space can feel barren, exposed, terrifying. But it is not empty. It is unclaimed.

For much of your life, loneliness may have triggered immediate escape. You didn't sit with it— you reacted to it. You filled every hour. You stayed busy. You chased stimulation, validation, conversation, attention. You reached outward not because you wanted intimacy, but because you needed relief. You scrolled until your mind blurred. You worked until exhaustion flattened you. You jumped into connection too quickly, mistaking proximity for safety. Those strategies made sense. They kept panic at bay. They kept the system regulated in the short term.

But they also taught your nervous system a dangerous lesson: loneliness is intolerable. Loneliness must be escaped. And anything that must be escaped becomes terrifying.

Healing asks you to learn a different relationship with this feeling. Not to romanticize it. Not to glorify solitude. But to stop treating loneliness like a personal failure or an emergency. To stop responding to it with self-erasure. Staying with loneliness does not mean isolating yourself or wallowing. It means refusing to abandon yourself when the feeling becomes uncomfortable. It means allowing the ache to exist without translating it into a story about your worth. It means noticing the sensations—the heaviness in the chest, the restlessness in the limbs, the quiet pressure behind the eyes—without immediately reaching for an exit.

At first, your body will resist. It will push you toward urgency. Toward action. Toward doing something to make the feeling stop. That urgency is not intuition. It is old wiring. It is the survival system trying to reassert control. And you do not have to obey it.

You can pause.
You can breathe.
You can let the moment exist without fixing it.

This is where self-trust begins to form—not in comfort, but in containment. When you stay long enough to discover that loneliness rises and falls like any other emotion. When you learn that it does not destroy you. When you experience yourself surviving the feeling without self-betrayal.

Loneliness becomes unbearable when you treat it as proof. Proof that you are unwanted. Proof that you are behind. Proof that you have failed at connection. But loneliness is often pointing toward something more precise: a need that deserves attention, not panic.

A longing that deserves curiosity, not suppression. What am I actually needing right now? Is it companionship, or is it reassurance? Is it being seen, or being soothed?

Is it grief asking to be felt? Is it rest?

Is it meaning?

When you stop reacting and start listening, loneliness becomes informative rather than overwhelming. Sometimes it is a cue to reach out with intention, not desperation. Sometimes it is a cue to create structure. Sometimes it is a cue to grieve honestly instead of trying to skip ahead. Sometimes it is simply a cue to sit quietly and allow the nervous system to recalibrate.

The strongest people are not the ones who never feel lonely. They are the ones who do not self- destruct when loneliness arrives. They do not turn the feeling into a frantic chase. They do not hand their stability to the next available distraction. They stay. They remain present. They allow the wave to move through without letting it dictate their behavior.

That staying builds something solid.

Loneliness begins to soften when your life contains meaning that does not hinge on constant connection. When you create rhythms that ground you. When you move your body and discharge stored stress. When you spend time outside and let your senses re-anchor you. When you cultivate friendships that do not demand performance. When you show up for yourself in quiet, consistent ways instead of waiting for rescue.

The strength of this work is invisible. It does not announce itself. It looks like evenings spent alone without spiraling. It looks like choosing sleep over scrolling. It looks like cooking for yourself even when your appetite is low. It looks like waking up and honoring one small commitment to yourself. These moments do not feel triumphant. But they are formative.

Because each time you stay, you teach your nervous system a new truth: I am not abandoned just because I am alone. You begin to experience solitude without collapse. You begin to trust that connection can be chosen rather than clung to.

Loneliness does not mean something is wrong with you. It means you are human, in transition, between chapters, learning to inhabit your life differently. And when you learn to be alone without abandoning yourself, love becomes an option rather than a necessity. Connection becomes something you meet with steadiness instead of hunger.

This is not the absence of longing. It is the end of panic. And that is where real healing begins.

Chapter 28

Chasing After Someone Who Has Chosen to Leave

There is a moment in many breakups that doesn't feel like sadness, it feels like free fall. One person shifts. Their tone changes. Their eyes stop searching yours. Their body turns slightly away, as if they are already halfway gone. And suddenly the world you were standing on—the assumptions, the routines, the future you thought you were walking toward—drops out from under you.

The mind tries to deny it at first. It reaches for logic, for explanations, for anything that will keep the ground intact. But the body knows faster than the mind. The body hears the threat before words are even spoken. The nervous system reads separation as danger. The attachment system goes into alarm. And a primitive, urgent command rises inside you: Stop this. Fix this. Don't let them leave.This is where chasing begins.

Not because you want to control anyone.
Not because you believe you are entitled to them.
Not because you are trying to manipulate.

But because panic has found the oldest wound in you and dug its fingers in.

When someone you love chooses to leave—emotionally, relationally, physically—it doesn't simply register as loss. It registers as *rejection*. And for someone with early abandonment wounds, rejection is never just rejection. It is a reopening. It is the body remembering every time love felt conditional, every time closeness was unstable, every time you were left holding the weight of someone else's decision.

The present moment becomes a portal. You are not just losing this person—you are reliving the original fear: *I am being left again.*

And when that fear floods the system, reasoning collapses. The brain searches for control the way a drowning person searches for air. You do not chase because it's strategic. You chase because the nervous system is screaming that stillness is unsafe. So you move.

You text.
You call.
You explain.
You apologize.
You promise.
You beg to be understood.
You offer change faster than change can be lived.
You revisit the same conversation with new wording, as if the right sentence could resurrect what is dying.

In the moment, it feels like devotion. It feels like love. It feels like courage. It feels like refusing to give up. But underneath all of it is the same raw truth: you are trying to stop pain by creating proximity.

Chasing is often misunderstood as weakness. But what it actually is, at its core, is a form of protest. It is the heart shouting through the throat. It is love mixed with terror, attachment mixed with desperation, longing mixed with survival.

It says:

Please don't leave me.
Please see how much you matter.
Please remember who we are.
Please, not like this. Please, not again.

And even when the words look calm on the screen, the energy beneath them is urgent. There is pressure in every message. A tightening. A grasping. The kind of emotional force that doesn't feel like force from the inside—because inside, it feels like trying not to die.
This is where the illusion of control begins to take over.

If I explain better...
If I say it more clearly...
If I show remorse in a way, they can't dismiss...

If I remind them of what we had...
If I prove I'm worth staying for...

Chasing convinces you that the relationship is a puzzle and the right combination of words will unlock it. It convinces you that if you just keep moving—keep reaching—keep trying—you can reverse what's happening.

But chasing rarely restores connection. It often accelerates distance.

Because once someone has chosen to step away, pursuit can land as pressure, even if it was born from pain. What you experience as love can be experienced by them as overwhelm. What you experience as persistence can be experienced by them as invasion. And the more you chase, the more their nervous system reinforces the decision to retreat.

This is the brutal paradox: the harder you try to hold on, the more you may push them further away.
Then the shame arrives.
It arrives in the quiet after the message is sent.
In the minutes you stare at the screen waiting for the typing bubble that never comes. In the hours you replay your own words and wonder why you couldn't stop.
In the morning after, when you wake up and remember what you did, and your stomach drops.

The Quiet That Raised Me

Shame doesn't just whisper. It accuses.

Why did I say that?
Why did I reach out again?
Why did I give them more access to my desperation?
Why did I abandon my dignity?

And the shame becomes its own wound. Not only are you losing the relationship—you are now losing your sense of self inside the loss.

But chasing does not mean you have no dignity. It means your nervous system was overwhelmed and trying to secure safety the only way it knew how: by pulling closeness toward you.

Understanding that doesn't excuse boundary violations. It doesn't erase the impact of repeated pursuit. It doesn't turn harm into innocence. But it tells the truth about the mechanism: this wasn't simply a "bad choice." It was a survival response colliding with grief.

Eventually—usually after enough silence, enough unanswered reaching, enough internal collapse—a turning point arrives.

Not a clean one. Not a confident one. A painful one.

You realize something that strips the illusion away:

150

You cannot convince someone to stay.

You cannot argue someone into wanting you. You cannot repair a relationship alone.

This realization burns because it exposes your powerlessness. And powerlessness, for a trauma- shaped system, can feel like humiliation. It can feel like death. It can feel like being a child again, small, unseen, waiting for someone else to decide whether you matter.Letting go of the chase means grieving more than the person. It means grieving the belief that effort alone could fix everything. It means grieving your fantasy of control. It means accepting limits you never wanted to accept.

This is where dignity begins to return—not as pride, but as *self-containment.*

Because when the pursuit stops, the energy that has been pouring outward has nowhere to go but back into you. And at first, that feels unbearable. The quiet becomes louder. The grief becomes sharper. The longing becomes physical.

But something else happens too: the nervous system starts to settle. The constant fight-or-flight begins to soften. Your mind stops rehearsing messages. Your body stops bracing for replies. You start to breathe again without realizing you had been holding your breath for days.

Space opens.

It doesn't feel like freedom at first. It feels like withdrawal.

Like detox.

Like your skin is missing.
But inside that space, self-respect can finally take root.
You begin to learn the difference between repair and pursuit. Repair requires two people turning toward the same fire.
Repair requires mutual willingness, mutual effort, mutual accountability. Repair has response. It has engagement. It has conversation that moves forward. Pursuit has repetition. It has one-sided reaching. It has silence in return. It has the slow erosion of self.

Learning the difference is brutal, but it is sacred. Because it protects you from spending your life proving yourself to someone who has already decided to look away.
Acceptance is not agreement. It is acknowledgement.

It is saying:

I don't want this. I hate this.
It breaks me.

But I will not cross my own boundaries to keep someone from leaving.

This is where healing begins to stand upright again. Not because the loss hurts less, but because you stop abandoning yourself inside the hurt.

Chasing someone who has chosen to leave does not mean you are weak. It means you were attached, afraid, and desperate to undo what felt unbearable.

Healing begins when you stop trying to persuade someone into staying and start learning how to stay with yourself, steady, honest, and intact.

Not in punishment.

Not in isolation.

But in dignity.

Because the moment you stop chasing is the moment you finally stop running after love at the cost of yourself.

Chapter 29

Forgiveness Without Forgetting Yourself

Forgiveness is often spoken about as if it is simple, clean, and morally required. As if it is something you reach for once enough time has passed, something you grant when you are tired of hurting, something that proves you are evolved or healed or spiritually mature. It is offered as an exit ramp from pain, a way to rise above what happened, a way to put the past neatly behind you.

But forgiveness is not neat. And for someone who has lived through trauma, loss, and the consequences of survival, forgiveness is never just about letting go. It is about *remembering without disappearing.*

For a long time, I thought forgiveness meant erasure. Erasing anger. Erasing memory. Erasing the parts of myself that still reacted, still ached, still tightened when I remembered. I thought forgiving meant becoming smaller around what hurt me, becoming quieter, becoming understanding enough that nothing could touch me anymore. I thought it meant being unaffected.

But forgiveness that requires you to shrink is not healing. Forgiveness that demands silence is not peace.

Forgiveness that skips over truth is not forgiveness at all. Real forgiveness begins where denial ends.

Many people reach for forgiveness too early, not because they are ready, but because the pain feels unbearable. They want relief. They want resolution. They want to stop replaying the story in their head. So they tell themselves they forgive before they have fully faced what happened. They bypass grief. They bypass anger. They bypass accountability. They tell themselves they are "over it" while their body is still bracing.

Premature forgiveness becomes another escape route. A way to avoid the hard work of feeling, naming, and integrating reality.

True forgiveness does not rush. It does not arrive on command. It waits until the truth has been faced fully and without distortion. It waits until you have allowed yourself to see the whole picture: what happened, what was lost, what cannot be undone, what hurt you, what you did in response to being hurt, and what was never yours to carry in the first place.

Only then does forgiveness stop being performative and start becoming grounded.

For people who were conditioned to prioritize others, forgiveness often turns into self-erasure. You learn early to understand everyone else before you understand yourself. You learn to contextualize harm. You learn to minimize impact. You learn to say, They did the best they could, even when what they did shattered something in you. You learn to excuse, explain, empathize, and absorb.

Understanding can be real and still incomplete.

You can understand why someone hurt you and still name that it hurt. You can see their limitations and still acknowledge the damage. Forgiveness does not require you to rewrite the story so that no one is responsible. It does not require you to reopen doors that were closed for good reason. It does not require you to restore access, closeness, or trust.

Forgiveness can exist alongside distance. It can exist alongside boundaries.

It can exist without reconciliation.

This is where many people get trapped believing that forgiving someone means returning to the same dynamic, offering the same access, risking the same harm. But forgiveness is not a bridge back.

It is a release forward. You can forgive someone and still decide that they no longer get to participate in your life. You can forgive and still protect yourself. You can forgive and still remember.

Self-forgiveness is often harder.

Because it forces you to stand in the places where you wish you had acted differently. It brings you face to face with the moments you regret, the choices you made while trying to survive, the ways you hurt others or yourself along the way. And the instinct is usually to swing to one of two extremes: either relentless self-punishment or total self-exoneration.

Neither leads to healing.

Self-forgiveness is not pretending the harm didn't happen. It is not rewriting your own history to feel better. It is the disciplined refusal to let your worst moments become your entire identity. It is the willingness to say, I see what I did. I take responsibility for it. I grieve the impact. And I am still allowed to grow beyond it.

That kind of forgiveness does not feel soft at first. It feels steady. It feels sobering. It asks you to hold accountability without turning it into self-destruction. It asks you to learn instead of collapse.

Memory plays a complicated role here. Many people

believe healing requires forgetting, but forgetting is not wisdom. Forgetting erases information. Memory, when integrated, becomes guidance. It teaches discernment. It sharpens boundaries. It keeps you from repeating what once harmed you.

The goal is not amnesia. The goal is proportion.
When you are not healed, memory traps you. You relive. You rehearse. You loop. The past feels present and consuming. When healing begins to take root, memory shifts. You remember without reliving. You reflect without being pulled under. The past becomes context rather than command.

This is how forgiveness becomes a boundary instead of a surrender.

One of the hardest truths to accept is that forgiveness does not automatically restore relationships. Reconciliation requires safety, mutual effort, and accountability on both sides. Forgiveness requires only honesty within yourself. You do not owe access to anyone who has shown they cannot handle it. You do not owe closeness to someone who continues to minimize or repeat harm.

Forgiveness does not demand that you return to what broke you.
Letting go is often misunderstood as approval. But

letting go is not agreement. It is the decision to stop carrying something that no longer deserves to occupy your nervous system. It is the choice to stop rehearsing the story in search of a different ending. It is the recognition that holding on is costing you more than releasing ever could.

This kind of release is quiet. It doesn't come with ceremony. It doesn't arrive all at once. Some days you feel free. Some days the resentment resurfaces. Both are part of the process.

Forgiveness is not a single act—it is a practice.

At its deepest level, forgiveness is not about the other person at all. It is about reclaiming your inner life. It is about refusing to let bitterness, shame, or self-contempt define the shape of your days. It is about choosing peace without pretending the pain never existed.

Forgiveness, when it is real, does not feel like relief washing over you. It feels like steadiness. Like something inside you finally stopped fighting.

Like you no longer need to prove how much it hurt to justify moving forward.

You remember.
You learn.
You release what no longer needs to be carried.

And you do not disappear in the process.

That is forgiveness without forgetting yourself.

Chapter 30

Learning to Trust Your Own Boundaries

For a long time, boundaries felt like betrayal. Not betrayal of other people—betrayal of safety, betrayal of belonging, betrayal of whatever fragile connection I had managed to hold together. I didn't grow up learning that limits could protect me. I grew up learning that limits could provoke. That saying no could trigger consequences. That asking for space could be interpreted as disrespect. That needing anything at all could turn me into a target. So I learned to survive without boundaries. I learned to swallow discomfort, bury my reactions, smile through tension, and call it strength. I learned to stay agreeable. To stay useful. To stay available. To stay quiet enough that no one would notice how much I was breaking.

And when you live like that long enough, you stop trusting yourself. Not because you lack instincts, but because you were trained to override them. Your body sends signals and you deny them. Your nervous system pulls back and you push forward. Your inner alarm flares and you explain it away. You learn to interpret your own needs as inconveniences and your own limits as weakness. You learn to abandon yourself in small ways so consistently that it starts to feel normal. Then one day you wake up and realize you are exhausted, resentful, and confused, because the truth is this: you have been crossing your own lines for years and calling it love.

Boundaries are not the harsh things I once imagined. They are not walls made of coldness. They are not weapons. They are not threats. They are not punishments. Boundaries are the quiet, fierce decisions that say: I will not participate in what harms me. I will not hand over access to parts of myself that are not safe to hold. I will not keep shrinking to keep someone else comfortable. I will not keep bleeding just to prove I can endure.

But to get there, you have to understand why boundaries felt impossible in the first place. If you grow up in an environment where your needs are dismissed, punished, laughed at, or weaponized against you, boundaries don't feel like tools. They feel like danger. You learn that speaking up leads to conflict. That honesty leads to retaliation. That discomfort is something you hide, because showing it makes you vulnerable. You learn to scan faces, measure moods, calculate timing, and adjust yourself before anyone has the chance to reject you. You become an expert in emotional weather. You feel shifts that no one else notices. You read pauses. You track tone. You pick up the tremor underneath a sentence that sounds harmless to everyone else. You become vigilant, hyperaware, constantly bracing.

That vigilance keeps you alive in childhood. But in adulthood, it becomes a cage. Because instead of learning how to set boundaries, you learn how to manage people. Instead of learning how to protect yourself, you learn how to anticipate reactions. Instead of learning how to say no, you learn how to twist yourself into whatever shape avoids fallout. It works until it doesn't. It works until your body starts protesting. It works until your mind starts breaking under the weight of what you've been tolerating. It works until resentment rises like heat in your chest and you don't even know why you're angry, because you've been trained to deny the very thing that would explain it: your limits were crossed, and you never defended them.

Boundary confusion shows up in adulthood in brutal, quiet ways. You over-explain. You apologize for needing space. You say yes when your whole body is saying no. You tolerate behavior that hurts you because you can't find the moment when you're "allowed" to stop it. You keep giving past your capacity, and then you suddenly disappear, not because you're cruel, but because you're depleted. You swing between over-giving and withdrawal, between caretaking and shutdown, between staying too long and leaving too fast. People call it inconsistency. But it isn't inconsistency. It's a nervous system that never learned how to hold a line safely. It's someone who never learned how to be firm without fear.

A boundary is not primarily something you tell other people. A boundary is something you recognize inside yourself first. It begins with awareness. With noticing. With listening. With taking your own signals seriously. Your body always knows before your mind can explain. Boundaries begin in sensation: the tightening in your chest when someone pushes. The ache in your stomach when you agree to something you don't want. The quiet dread when someone texts and you feel obligated instead of willing. The irritation that flares when you keep being interrupted. The exhaustion that hits when you keep giving and no one notices the cost. These sensations are not flaws. They are information. They are your internal compass trying to guide you back to yourself.

Learning to trust your boundaries means learning to stop arguing with that information. It means learning to stop gaslighting your own discomfort. It means refusing to treat your instincts like they are irrational just because someone else benefits from you ignoring them.

This is where self-trust begins to rebuild—not in grand declarations, but in small, deliberate acts. You pause before you answer. You breathe before you agree. You give yourself permission to check in. You stop performing automatic availability. You stop treating your "yes" as something you owe.

You start asking, quietly but firmly:

Do I want to do this?
Do I have the capacity for this?
Does this feel safe?
Does this feel aligned?
Does this feel like self-respect or self- abandonment?

At first, that pause feels uncomfortable. It can feel selfish. It can trigger guilt. It can trigger fear. Because you've been trained to believe that other people's needs are emergencies and your needs are optional. You've been trained to confuse compliance with kindness. You've been trained to confuse self-erasure with love. So when you finally start listening to yourself, it can feel wrong—not because it is wrong, but because it is new. Your nervous system is adjusting to a reality where protecting yourself does not automatically mean being abandoned.

And then comes the hardest part: boundaries require action. Not just awareness, not just insight—action. They require you to stop. To say no. To step back. To disappoint someone sometimes. To tolerate the discomfort of holding your line when someone pushes against it. Because boundaries don't become real when you understand them.

They become real when you enforce them.

A boundary is clarity, not control. It is not about changing another person. It is about deciding what you will participate in and what you will not. It is about recognizing what you can offer and what you cannot. It is about naming your limits without begging permission to have them.

A boundary sounds like: I'm not available for that. It sounds like: I need time before I respond.

It sounds like: I'm not comfortable continuing this conversation.

It sounds like: If the tone stays like this, I'm going to step away.

It sounds like: I care about you, and I am not doing this.

It sounds like: No.

No explanation. No defense. No courtroom presentation of your pain. No frantic attempt to be understood. Clarity. Clean. Direct. Steady.

But if you've spent your life over-explaining, boundaries will feel like walking into a room without armor. You will want to justify yourself. You will want to soften it.

You will want to turn your boundary into an apology. You will want to add extra words so no one can accuse you of being mean. You will want to negotiate against yourself. And that is the old pattern trying to survive. That is the old fear trying to keep you safe by making you small again.

Learning to trust your boundaries means learning to hold them without performing guilt. Without asking for permission. Without waiting for someone else to validate your need. Because if your boundaries only exist when someone agrees with them, they are not boundaries. They are requests. And requests can be ignored.

Boundaries become real when you are willing to enforce them even when someone is disappointed, even when someone is confused, even when someone tries to guilt you, even when someone claims you've changed. Especially when someone claims you've changed. Because you have. You are changing from someone who abandons themselves to someone who stands with themselves.

This is where relationships start revealing their true architecture. Some relationships improve when boundaries enter. They breathe. They stabilize. They become clearer. People who respect you will adjust. They may not always like it, but they will listen. They will take you seriously.

They will care about your capacity. They will stop treating your availability like an entitlement.

Other relationships will resist. Not because your boundary is wrong, but because the relationship was built around you having fewer limits. Some people benefit from your silence. Some people depend on your over-functioning. Some people are comfortable with you as long as you stay easy, accessible, accommodating. When you begin to hold a line, they feel it as a threat. Not because you are attacking them, but because you are no longer abandoning yourself to keep them comfortable. That resistance can hurt. It can trigger the old wound that says: If I protect myself, I will be left. If I say no, I will be punished. If I hold a limit, I will lose love. And this is where boundaries become more than a relationship skill. They become a spiritual act of self-loyalty. They become proof that you can stay with yourself even if someone else doesn't like it.

Trusting your boundaries means learning to stand with yourself in that moment. It means letting discomfort rise without surrendering your line. It means feeling guilty without reversing your decision. It means tolerating someone's disappointment without collapsing into self-doubt. It means allowing the nervous system to shake and settle and learn something new: I can set a limit and survive the feeling that follows.

At first, boundaries feel like conflict even when you deliver them calmly. At first, your body will interpret holding a boundary as danger. You will feel adrenaline. You will feel heat. You will feel the urge to fix it. You will want to reach back out and make it okay. And if you can resist that urge—if you can hold steady—something important happens. You teach your nervous system that self-protection is not the same as abandonment. You teach yourself that you can be loving and firm at the same time.

And then something else begins to change. You start recognizing resentment sooner. You start catching the moment you begin to overextend. You start noticing when your yes is forced. You start feeling the difference between generosity and obligation. You start choosing differently in real time instead of only realizing afterward that you've betrayed yourself again.

This is the quiet revolution: you begin to become trustworthy to yourself.

Because self-trust is not a feeling. It is evidence. It is built through follow-through. Every time you honor your own limit, you create proof. Every time you say no and survive, you create proof. Every time you step away from what drains you, you create proof. Every time you stop explaining and simply hold your line, you create proof. And slowly, that evidence begins to rewrite the old belief that you must abandon yourself to be loved.

Boundaries, when trusted, become the foundation of real connection. Not the enemy of intimacy, the architecture of it. Without boundaries, you don't have closeness; you have enmeshment. You have overextension. You have hidden resentment. You have quiet self-erasure that eventually erupts or collapses. Boundaries bring clarity. They reduce confusion. They create safety. They make room for authenticity because you no longer have to pretend, you're okay when you're not. You no longer have to perform endless capacity. You can show up as a whole person—limited, honest, human.

And there is a suspenseful truth here that many people avoid until life forces them to face it: the more you trust your boundaries, the more you stop chasing approval. You stop negotiating for permission to exist. You stop living like love is something you must earn through endurance.

You begin living like love is something that must be compatible with self-respect.

That shift changes everything. It changes who you let close. It changes what you tolerate. It changes how you speak. It changes how you leave. It changes how you stay.

Because when you trust your boundaries, you stop asking: What will they think? And you start asking, What will I lose if I abandon myself again?

And once you ask that question honestly, you cannot unsee the answer.

You begin to understand that boundaries are not the reason relationships fall apart. Boundaries reveal what was already unstable. Boundaries expose what was already unbalanced. Boundaries illuminate who is capable of meeting you in mutual respect and who was only comfortable with you when you were easy to use.

This is painful. And it is also liberating.

Because the goal is not to keep everyone. The goal is to keep yourself. To stop crossing your own lines in the name of love.

To stop shrinking in the name of peace. To stop bleeding in the name of loyalty. To stop calling self-betrayal a virtue.

Learning to trust your boundaries is learning to trust your own life. It is learning to believe that your limits matter. That your energy matters. That your "no" matters. That your yes should be clean, not coerced. That your inner signals are not inconveniences—they are guidance.

Over time, boundaries stop feeling like walls and start feeling like anchors. They hold you steady when old patterns try to pull you back into performance. They keep you grounded when fear tells you to chase. They protect the tender parts of you that used to be sacrificed first. They make your life clearer. They make your relationships cleaner. They make your self-respect real.

And the most powerful part is this: once you trust your boundaries, you no longer must be at war inside yourself. You stop negotiating against your own needs. You stop overriding your own body. You stop disappearing in small ways all day long.

You begin to stand, firmly, quietly, in your own life.

And that is what healing looks like when it becomes lived instead of imagined.

Chapter 31

What Healing Actually Looks Like Over Time

For a long time, I thought healing would announce itself. I imagined a moment when something would click, when the weight would lift, when the past would finally loosen its grip and release me. I believed healing would feel clean and obvious, like crossing a finish line and knowing, without question, that I had arrived. But healing does not arrive that way. It does not knock. It does not declare victory. Most of the time, healing happens quietly, without witnesses, without certainty, without applause. It happens in the middle of ordinary days, in moments so small they almost feel unworthy of attention. And yet, those moments change everything.

Healing is not a straight line. It is not a dramatic transformation. It does not erase what happened or undo the ways the past shaped you. It moves slowly, unevenly, sometimes so subtly that you don't notice it until you look back and realize something fundamental has shifted. You still carry the memories. You still feel the echoes. You still have days when old fears rise fast and familiar. The difference is not that those experiences disappear. The difference is that they no longer own you.

Early on, emotional loops feel endless. You replay conversations. You rehearse regrets. You spiral into self-criticism. You analyze every reaction, every misstep, every feeling that feels too big or too much. It can feel like you are trapped inside your own mind, circling the same terrain again and again, searching for relief. Over time, though, something begins to change. The loops start to shorten. You still get triggered, but you recover faster. You still feel shame, but you recognize it sooner. You still feel fear, but it no longer dictates every decision. This shortening of the loop is not dramatic, but it is profound. It is one of the clearest signs that healing is actually happening.

You begin to notice pauses where there used to be only reaction. A breath appears where panic once lived. A moment of awareness interrupts an automatic response. You might still feel the urge to withdraw, to chase, to explain, to numb, to control. But now, instead of being swept away by it, you see it. You feel it rise. You recognize the pattern activating. And sometimes just sometimes, you choose differently. That pause is fragile at first. It might last only a second. But it is powerful. It creates space, and in that space, you regain agency.

Healing also changes your relationship with discomfort. It does not make life painless. It makes you more capable. You learn how to tolerate emotional weather without panicking. You learn how to sit with sadness without immediately trying to escape it. You learn how to feel loneliness without reaching for the nearest distraction. You learn how to hold guilt without collapsing into self-punishment. You learn how to feel longing without acting impulsively. Emotions begin to move through you instead of overwhelming you. They rise, peak, and soften when allowed space. You discover, often with surprise, that you can survive feelings you once believed would destroy you.

Another quiet shift takes place in how you speak to yourself. The internal voice that once attacked relentlessly begins to soften. It does not disappear, but it loses some of its authority. Instead of immediately asking, "What's wrong with me?" you begin to ask, "What's happening for me right now?" This change matters deeply. It transforms self-reflection from a trial into a conversation. Compassion becomes more consistent, less conditional. You stop treating yourself like a problem to be solved and start treating yourself like someone worth understanding.

Healing shows up in daily choices, not grand gestures. It shows up when you choose rest instead of overexertion. When you stop a spiral before it gains momentum. When you tell the truth even though it feels uncomfortable. When you set a boundary without apologizing for it. When you notice that you need support, allow yourself to ask. When you resist the urge to chase validation.

When you let yourself be imperfect without immediately punishing yourself for it.

None of these moments look heroic. But together, they reshape the architecture of your life.

Perhaps the most meaningful change is the slow rebuilding of self-trust. Trauma fractures that trust. It teaches you that your emotions are dangerous, your instincts unreliable, your needs inconvenient. Healing repairs that fracture one small promise at a time. You begin to trust that you can handle your emotions without being consumed by them. You begin to trust that you can pause instead of react. You begin to trust that you can make mistakes and repair them. This trust is not bravado or confidence. It is reliability. It is knowing that you will show up for yourself even when things are hard.

Healing is not linear, and it never will be. There are days that feel like setbacks. Old memories surface unexpectedly. Grief returns without warning. Certain triggers still sting. This does not erase progress. Healing unfolds in spirals, not straight lines. You revisit old themes with new awareness. Each return is gentler, wiser, less consuming. What feels like regression is often integration happening beneath the surface. You are not starting over. You are deepening.

Over time, a quieter, stronger self begins to emerge. You

Shawn M. Mack

stop fighting yourself. You stop demanding perfection. You stop measuring progress by how little you feel pain. You stop waiting to feel "fixed." Instead, you begin to live. You make room for joy without guilt. You allow rest without justification. You accept complexity without shame. You become steadier— not because life has become easier, but because you are more grounded within it.

Healing does not change who you were. It changes how you relate to who you were. You no longer see your past only as damage. You begin to see it as context. You understand the forces that shaped you without letting them dictate your future. You carry your history with awareness instead of resistance. The energy once spent running, hiding, or fighting turns inward and becomes presence.

What healing actually looks like over time is subtle but unmistakable. It looks like fewer emergencies inside your body. It looks like calmer responses to things that once sent you into collapse or chaos. It looks like a growing ability to stay with yourself through discomfort instead of abandoning yourself to escape it. It looks like a life that feels less dramatic but more real.

There is no moment when you are finished. Healing is not something you complete. It is something you live. It reveals itself in how you respond, how you pause, how you choose, and how you treat yourself when no one else is watching. It is not fast. It is not flashy. It is not linear. But it is real.

And over time, it becomes the quiet foundation beneath everything you build next.

Chapter 32

Becoming Someone You Can Stand Behind

There comes a moment in healing when the questions change. It stops being about what went wrong and starts becoming about what comes next. Not in theory. Not in fantasy. But in the quiet, unglamorous reality of daily life. The question sharpens and refuses to leave: who am I choosing to be now, when no one is watching, when there is no crisis to distract me, when there is no audience to impress. Becoming someone you can stand behind is not a declaration. It is a reckoning.

For a long time, survival shaped my identity. I reacted. I adapted. I endured. I learned how to perform competence, confidence, intensity, and strength. I learned how to manage perception. I learned how to look functional even when everything inside me was fractured. That version of me got things done. He survived. He pushed forward. But survival is not the same as integrity. Survival asks only one thing: get through this. Integrity asks something harder: live in a way that does not require you to look away from yourself afterward.

Becoming someone you can stand behind begins with closing the distance between values and behavior. That distance is where shame grows. That distance is where self-respect erodes. You can say the right things, understand the right concepts, even feel remorse—but if your actions continue to contradict what you claim matters, something inside you stays unsettled. Healing narrows that gap slowly, painfully, deliberately. You begin to notice the moments where you are tempted to betray yourself for comfort, approval, or relief. You feel the pull to explain, to justify, to escape, to overextend. And sometimes, you stop.

Integrity does not arrive as perfection. It arrives as restraint. It shows up when you pause instead of reacting. When you tell the truth even though it costs you comfort. When you resist the urge to chase validation. When you choose to walk away from something familiar but harmful. These choices are not dramatic. They are quiet. They rarely earn praise. But they accumulate. Over time, they build something solid inside you. a sense that your life is starting to make sense from the inside out.

For much of my life, I cared deeply about how I was seen. That focus made sense. When safety is conditional, image becomes armor. Approval becomes currency. Being perceived as good, capable, or desirable feels like protection. But image is unstable. It shifts with circumstance. It depends on others. Healing slowly moves the center of gravity inward. The question changes from how am I perceived to can I respect myself when I look honestly at my choices. That question is harder to evade. It does not respond to charm or explanation. It responds only to consistency.

Living in alignment does not mean you never falter. It means you notice sooner when you do. It means you correct course without collapsing into shame or hiding behind excuses. You stop measuring yourself in extremes, good or bad, healed or broken and start measuring yourself by effort, awareness, and repair. You ask yourself difficult questions without cruelty. Where did I drift today. Where did I stay grounded. Where did I choose fear, and where did I choose integrity. This kind of reflection is firm, but it is not punishing. It is how accountability becomes sustainable.

Growth, at this stage, is often invisible to others. It does not announce itself. It does not come with dramatic confrontations or sweeping transformations. It looks like not sending the text you want to send. It looks like holding a boundary calmly. It looks like tolerating discomfort without numbing it. It looks like choosing honesty over performance. These moments do not feel heroic. They feel uncomfortable. But they are the moments that reshape identity. They teach you who you are becoming.

One of the most important shifts is learning how to hold yourself accountable without cruelty. Harsh self-judgment feels productive, but it actually drives fear. Fear leads to hiding. Hiding erodes integrity. Accountability paired with compassion does the opposite. It creates safety to be honest. You can say I didn't handle that well without saying I am irredeemable. You can acknowledge harm without destroying yourself to prove remorse. This balance is not weakness. It is maturity.

Living with integrity also requires choosing the long view. It means thinking beyond immediate relief and short-term comfort. It means asking what kind of person you want to be years from now, not just what will soothe you today. This does not require rigidity or moral purity. It requires direction. You begin to orient your life around values instead of impulses. You stop negotiating against yourself. You start choosing actions you can live with afterward.

As integrity deepens, something subtle happens: you begin to trust yourself again. Not because you are perfect, but because you are consistent. When you say you will pause before reacting and you actually pause. When you say you will tell the truth and you do. When you say you will take care of yourself and you follow through. Each small act becomes evidence. Over time, that evidence rebuilds trust. And self-trust is stabilizing in a way nothing external can be.

To stand behind your life does not mean approving of every chapter. It means owning your story without running from it. It means allowing complexity. Holding regret and growth at the same time. It means accepting that you are unfinished—and choosing to live responsibly anyway. You stop trying to outrun who you were. You stop trying to perform who you think you should be.

You begin to inhabit who you are, honestly, imperfectly, deliberately.

Becoming someone you can stand behind is not a destination you reach. It is a practice you return to. It happens in ordinary moments, when no one is watching, when choices are small and unremarkable. It grows through restraint, honesty, humility, and patience. And over time, it creates something quietly powerful inside you: the ability to live with yourself.

Not because you are flawless.

But because you are paying attention.

Because you are choosing integrity over impulse.

Because you are becoming someone whose life you no longer need to escape. And that, more than anything else, is what makes healing real.

Chapter 33

Living With Integrity, Not Perfection

For a long time, I believed integrity meant flawlessness. I thought it meant never slipping, never contradicting myself, never showing the parts of me that were still uncertain or afraid. Any mistake felt like proof that I hadn't really changed, that the work hadn't taken, that I was still the same person pretending to be better. That belief kept me locked in quiet tension, constantly monitoring myself, bracing for failure, measuring every reaction as if one wrong move could undo everything. What I didn't understand then was that perfection is rigid, and rigidity is just another form of fear. Integrity, by contrast, is alive.

Living with integrity does not require purity. It requires honesty. It requires the willingness to see yourself clearly, even when what you see is uncomfortable. Perfection demands control; integrity demands presence. Perfection asks you to eliminate contradiction; integrity asks you to hold it without lying about it. When I stopped trying to be fixed and started trying to be truthful, something loosened inside me. The pressure to perform healing disappeared, and in its place came a steadier responsibility: to show up as I am and take ownership of what I do next.

The urge to be "done" with growth is seductive. After so much pain and reflection, it is tempting to want a finish line, a moment of arrival where you are finally beyond the patterns, beyond the fear, beyond the mistakes. But healing does not remove your humanity. Trying to become finished often recreates the very conditions that caused harm in the first place—suppression, self-policing, the refusal to admit weakness. Integrity begins the moment you stop asking yourself to be flawless and start asking yourself to be real.

Integrity is built in ordinary moments, not grand gestures. It lives in the quiet decisions no one applauds. It shows up when you slow down instead of reacting, when you tell the truth instead of shaping a story that protects your image, when you admit you're overwhelmed instead of pretending you're fine. It shows up when you apologize without defending yourself, when you set a limit even though it disappoints someone, when you keep a promise, you made to yourself even when no one else would know if you broke it. These moments do not look impressive. They do not announce transformation. But they quietly form a life that feels internally coherent.

You will still fall short. That is not a failure of integrity; it is the terrain integrity operates in. You will misjudge situations. You will react emotionally.

You will say things you wish you had said differently. The difference is not the absence of these moments, but how you respond to them.

Integrity does not spiral into shame or hide behind denial. It stays present. It says I see what happened. I take responsibility. I want to do better next time. This response keeps growth intact even when mistakes happen. It turns failure into information instead of identity.

As integrity deepens, the need to prove yourself begins to fade. You stop narrating your progress. You stop explaining yourself excessively. You stop trying to convince others that you are good, changed, or worthy. Not because you don't care, but because your sense of worth no longer depends on constant validation. Your actions begin to speak for themselves, and that quiet consistency carries more weight than any performance ever could.

One of the most misunderstood aspects of integrity is its relationship with self-compassion. Many people believe that being kind to yourself will make you complacent, that without harsh self-criticism, you will lose motivation. The opposite is true. Self-compassion creates the safety required for honest accountability. When you stop attacking yourself, you free up energy for change. You can look at your behavior clearly without collapsing under it. You can hold yourself to a standard without turning that standard into a weapon. This balance—firm and humane at the same time—is the core of integrity.

Living with integrity also means accepting contradiction. You can be healed and still healing. You can be wise and still unsure. You can carry regret and still move forward. Integrity does not erase these tensions; it integrates them. It allows you to live with complexity rather than fighting it. You stop demanding that your life make sense in simple terms and start allowing it to be honest instead.

Choosing integrity is choosing a long path. It is not a moment of clarity; it is a way of moving through the world. It shows up in how you handle discomfort, how you treat people when no one is watching, how you speak to yourself when you fall short, how you keep going when progress feels slow. This path is not glamorous, but it is solid. Over time, it builds something quietly powerful: self-respect.

When your actions begin to align with your values, life feels less chaotic. Decisions become simpler. Inner conflict softens. You stop negotiating against yourself. You may still struggle, but you are no longer at war inside. That alignment creates a kind of peace that does not depend on outcomes or approval. It comes from knowing that, even on difficult days, you are trying to live in a way that makes sense to you.

Living with integrity is not about becoming better than you were. It is about becoming more honest, more grounded, and more responsible with the life you are living now. It is choosing consistency over perfection, presence over performance, truth over image. It is learning to live in a way that does not require constant justification or escape.

And when you live this way long enough, something changes quietly but decisively. You begin to trust the person you are becoming. You stop chasing a version of yourself that never existed. You stand inside your life instead of hovering above it, waiting to approve or condemn.

You live with awareness, with restraint, with intention.

Not perfectly.

But honestly.

And that honesty becomes the foundation you no longer have to outrun.

Chapter 34

The Moment I Stopped Begging the Fire

There comes a moment, not dramatic, not announced, not witnessed when a person realizes they have been negotiating with something that was never meant to keep them warm. I didn't arrive at that moment through clarity or courage. I arrived there through exhaustion. The kind that sinks into your bones and makes hope feel heavy instead of alive. The kind that whispers not quite, but enough. Enough pleading with flames to become shelter. Enough translating pain into patience. Enough convincing myself that if I could just say it better, love would finally stay.

For most of my life, I believed intensity meant intimacy. If something burned hot enough, it had to be real. If it hurt deeply, it had to matter. I confused chaos for chemistry, distance for depth, unpredictability for passion. I learned early that love came with conditions and silence came before impact, so I learned to lean in harder when others pulled away. I learned to prove instead of pause. To overexplain instead of observe. To chase instead of choosing myself. I didn't know I was reenacting an old survival script. I only knew that walking away felt like dying, and staying felt like disappearing.

I begged the fire because I was taught that warmth was earned through endurance. If I could withstand the heat, I would eventually be rewarded with closeness. But fire does not evolve into safety. It consumes, or it leaves ash. And every time I reached for it, I lost another piece of myself, telling the same lie in a different voice: maybe this time will be different. Maybe this time I'll finally be enough.

The truth arrived quietly. It didn't shout. It didn't accuse. It simply stood there while I watched myself bending into shapes that weren't human anymore. Smaller. Quieter. More careful. Less honest. Less alive. I saw how much energy I was spending trying to be chosen by people who were already telling me no through their absence, their inconsistency, their half-commitments. I saw how often I mistook anxiety for connection and longing for love. And something in me finally refused to keep bleeding for a lesson I had already learned.

Stopping didn't feel empowering at first. It felt terrifying. The silence after I stepped back was deafening. Without the chase, there was nowhere to hide from myself. No drama to distract me. No emotional emergencies to manage. Just me and the space I had been avoiding my entire life. And in that space, grief rose up, not just for the relationship, but for every version of me that thought survival was the same thing as love.

I grieved the boy who learned to scan rooms instead of resting in them. I grieved the man who thought being wanted required constant performance. I grieved the belief that if someone pulled away, it meant I should try harder. I grieved the years I spent translating rejection into motivation and abandonment into a challenge. None of that made me strong. It only made me tired.

This chapter was not about closure. It was about consent. About withdrawing my energy from battles I was never meant to fight. About choosing not to participate in dynamics that required me to abandon myself just to feel close to someone else. I didn't become colder. I became clearer. I didn't stop loving. I stopped setting myself on fire to prove that I could.

The moment I stopped begging for the fire was the moment I understood that real connection does not require pursuit. It does not demand shrinking. It does not punish honesty. Love that is meant for you does not make you feel like you are constantly auditioning for permanence. It meets you. It steadies you. It stays.

And in the quiet aftermath, something unexpected happened. The space I feared began to feel like ground. Solid. Supportive. Mine. For the first time, I wasn't chasing warmth. I was learning how to generate it from within. Not loudly.

Not dramatically. But steadily. Safely. Without burning myself alive to feel seen. That was the moment everything changed. Not because someone finally chose me, but because I stopped choosing pain just to avoid being alone.

Chapter 35

What I Built After the Noise

After the fire, there was quiet. Not the sharp, threatening silence I grew up bracing for, not the kind that made my muscles tense and my thoughts race, but a wide, unfamiliar stillness that didn't ask anything of me. At first, I didn't trust it. I kept waiting for the other shoe to drop, for the calm to reveal itself as another trick, another pause before impact. But nothing came. The quiet stayed. And slowly, reluctantly, I stayed with it.

I didn't rebuild my life all at once. There was no dramatic reinvention, no sudden clarity that rearranged everything overnight. What I built came together the way a body heals after years of holding its breath, inch by inch, moment by moment, with setbacks that felt like failures until I understood they were just part of learning how to live without constant alarm. I started with small, almost invisible acts of loyalty to myself. Going to bed when I was tired instead of scrolling to outrun my thoughts. Saying no without explaining. Letting unanswered messages remain unanswered. Trusting that I did not owe my nervous system perpetual stimulation to prove I was alive.

The noise I walked away from had once felt essential. Chaos gave me direction. Urgency gave me purpose. Being needed even in unhealthy ways made me feel real. Without it, I had to confront an unsettling truth: I didn't actually know who I was when no one was pulling on me. When there was no conflict to manage, no distance to close, no emotional weather to predict, I felt exposed. Stripped of my old roles, I had to meet myself without performance, without strategy, without armor.

What emerged wasn't dramatic. It was grounded. I learned the difference between peace and emptiness, between boredom and rest. I learned that calm doesn't mean something is missing; it means nothing is threatening me. That realization alone rewired something deep inside me. My body began to unlearn the belief that love arrives with tension. My mind started to release the idea that anticipation is the same thing as connection. I stopped confusing longing with depth. I stopped calling instability passion.

I built boundaries the way you build muscle slowly, with effort, sometimes shaking under the weight of guilt. Every time I chose myself, there was a moment of fear that followed. Fear that I was being selfish. Fear that I was becoming distant. Fear that without my over-giving, I would be forgotten. But the more consistently I honored my limits, the more I realized how much of my past closeness had been fueled by obligation, not mutual desire. The people who disappeared when I stopped overextending were never anchored to me in the first place.

In the quiet, I started listening differently. Not just to others, but to myself. I noticed how my body reacted to certain names, certain memories, certain expectations. Tightness became information. Fatigue became a message. Relief became a compass. I stopped overriding these signals in the name of being agreeable, understanding, or low maintenance. I let my intuition speak without cross-examining it. And for the first time, I trusted what it said.

What I built after the noise was not a wall. It was a foundation. One that could hold joy without bracing for loss. One that could experience closeness without losing itself. I learned that safety isn't the absence of conflict; it's the presence of repair, consistency, and choice. I learned that love does not need to be earned through endurance. It needs to be offered freely and received without fear.

There were moments I missed the old intensity. Not because it was good, but because it was familiar. Healing has a way of feeling lonely before it feels liberating. But each time I was tempted to return to the noise, I remembered the cost. The sleepless nights. The self-doubt disguised as devotion. The way I used to disappear inside relationships, while calling it loyalty. I remembered who I had to betray to keep those dynamics alive.

I kept building. A life where my nervous system could rest. A sense of self that didn't hinge on being chosen. A version of connection that didn't require urgency to feel meaningful.

I didn't become perfect. I became present.
I didn't erase my past. I integrated it.
I didn't harden. I stabilized.

What I built after the noise was not flashy or impressive to the outside world. But it was solid. It was mine. And for the first time, I wasn't surviving my life, I was inhabiting it.

Chapter 36

The Day I Stopped Asking to Be Held and Learned How to Stand

There was a day not marked by dates or witnesses—when I realized I had spent most of my life asking to be held by people who were never standing on solid ground themselves. I wasn't asking for too much. I was asking the wrong people. I mistook collapse for closeness, thought shared wounds were the same as shared direction, believed that if we leaned hard enough into each other, neither of us would fall. But two people reaching for balance at the same time don't create stability. They create sway. And eventually, they both go down.

I had learned early that attachment meant survival. That connection was something you clung to, not something you trusted. So I built my sense of safety around proximity around being needed, being chosen, being indispensable. If someone leaned on me, I felt real. If they drifted, I panicked. I didn't know how to stand without someone else pressing against me, didn't know how to feel grounded unless another heartbeat was close enough to regulate my own. I called that love. It was dependence dressed up as devotion.

Standing on my own felt like betrayal at first. As if I were abandoning a sacred role I'd been trained to play: the one who absorbs, adapts, rescues, endures. The one who stays steady so others don't have to. Letting go of that identity felt like letting go of purpose. Who was I if I wasn't holding everything together? Who was I if I wasn't the calm inside someone else's storm? The fear wasn't that I would be alone. The fear was that I would be unnecessary.

Learning to stand required a kind of courage I didn't know I had. Not the loud, defiant kind. The quiet, disciplined kind. The kind that shows up every day and resists old instincts. The kind that chooses pause over pursuit, truth over reassurance, alignment over attachment. I had to feel my own weight for the first time—feel where I was weak, where I was strong, where I was still healing. I had to stop outsourcing my sense of safety to other people's availability.

There were moments my legs shook. Moments when the old reflex to reach out flared up, sharp and convincing. Moments when standing alone felt like exposure, like standing in open air without armor. But each time I resisted the urge to collapse into someone else, something inside me strengthened. Not dramatically. Gradually. My spine learned what it meant to support me.

My breath slowed. My thoughts stopped racing ahead to imagined abandonment. I discovered that I could be steady without being rigid, independent without being isolated.

I stopped asking people to hold me up and started asking myself harder questions. Does this connection move in the same direction I do? Does it offer consistency, not just intensity? Do I feel clearer or smaller after engaging? Am I standing beside this person, or am I bracing for them? These questions changed everything. They filtered out dynamics built on urgency and revealed those rooted in mutual respect. I no longer confused being wanted with being compatible.

Standing didn't make me colder. It made me selective. It didn't close my heart. It protected it. I learned that real intimacy happens when two people can stand fully on their own and still choose closeness not out of fear, not out of lack, but out of alignment. I learned that support feels different when it's offered between equals instead of extracted through need. There is no desperation in it. No silent bargaining. Just presence, freely given.

The day I learned how to stand was the day I stopped asking relationships to save me. I stopped handing over responsibility for my stability, my worth, my sense of direction. I took it back— awkwardly at first, then with growing confidence. I realized I didn't need to be held to be safe. I needed to be rooted. I needed to trust myself enough to stay upright even when someone else chose not to stay.

And from that place steady, grounded, intact, and I discovered a new kind of strength. One that doesn't announce itself. One that doesn't chase validation. One that doesn't crumble when someone walks away. I wasn't standing against anyone. I was standing for myself. And in that stance, I finally understood: the strongest connections don't come from leaning. They come from choosing to walk side by side, fully supported by your own ground.

Chapter 37

The Kind of Love That Doesn't Ask You to Disappear

For a long time, I believed love was something you survived. Something you endured, adapted to, negotiated with. I thought love required a quiet erasure of needs, of instincts, of parts of yourself that made other people uncomfortable. I thought if I could just soften enough, bend enough, become easier to hold, then love would finally stay. What I didn't understand was that anything that asks you to disappear is not love. It's fear wearing intimacy's clothes.

I didn't lose myself all at once. I disappeared in pieces. A preference here. A boundary there. A truth swallowed to keep the peace. I told myself these were compromises, signs of maturity, evidence that I was learning how to love better. But compromise that only moves in one direction is not growth. It's abandonment—quiet, gradual, and devastating. And I became so skilled at it that I stopped noticing when I was the one being left behind.

The shift didn't happen because I met someone new. It happened because I finally met myself without rushing past the discomfort. I noticed how often I felt tension in my chest when I was with certain people. How my words became measured, my emotions filtered, my joy dimmed just enough to avoid being "too much." I noticed how relief—not excitement—was my dominant feeling after some interactions. Relief that I hadn't asked for too much. Relief that I hadn't caused conflict. Relief that I was still accepted. That wasn't love. That was self-monitoring disguised as connection.

I began to understand that the right kind of love doesn't require translation. You don't have to explain your tone, justify your feelings, or shrink your needs into something more palatable. The right kind of love makes room instead of demands reduction. It doesn't punish honesty or reward silence. It doesn't make you choose between being real and being kept. It doesn't ask you to betray yourself just to belong.

This realization was both liberating and sobering. Liberating because it named what I had been feeling all along. Sobering because it meant I could no longer pretend I didn't know the difference. I could no longer romanticize inconsistency or call emotional distance "depth." I had to stop mistaking anxiety for passion and longing for intimacy. I had to admit that some of what I called love was actually me trying to earn safety in familiar ways.

The kind of love I began to imagine, then slowly require and felt quieter than what I was used to. Not dull. Not flat. Just steady. It didn't spike my nervous system or keep me guessing. It didn't arrive with urgency or threats of loss. It showed up consistently, without performance. And at first, that scared me. Chaos had always been my reference point. Calm felt suspicious. But over time, my body learned the truth before my mind fully caught up: safety is not boring. It's regulating. It's spacious. It lets you breathe.

I stopped chasing connections that needed me to contort myself to fit. I stopped explaining my worth to people committed to misunderstanding me. I stopped mistaking intensity for investment. And in doing so, I created space for something entirely different—not just with others, but within myself. I began offering myself the same presence I had been giving away so freely. I listened. I rested. I told the truth, even when it risked disapproval.

The kind of love that doesn't ask you to disappear starts with you staying. Staying with your feelings instead of overriding them. Staying with your boundaries instead of apologizing for them. Staying with your voice even when it shakes. It grows in environments where consistency replaces confusion and where care doesn't have to be proven through pain. It is built, not chased. Chosen, not extracted.

I don't know exactly when that love will meet me in another person. But I know this: I will recognize it by how intact I feel in its presence. By how little effort it takes to remain myself. By how my nervous system settles instead of spirals. And until that love arrives externally, I am no longer willing to abandon myself internally. I have learned the cost of disappearing. I have learned the price of staying silent to be kept.

This time, I choose the kind of love that lets me exist fully.

Unedited. Unafraid. Still here.

Chapter 38

When I No Longer Mistook Familiar Pain for Home

For a long time, I called certain feelings "home" simply because they were familiar. The tension. The waiting. The constant scanning for shifts in tone or distance. I didn't question why my body stayed braced even in moments that were supposed to feel safe. I just assumed that love came with vigilance, that closeness required alertness, that rest was something you earned after surviving someone else's moods. I didn't realize I was mistaking old pain for belonging.

Familiar pain is seductive. It speaks in a voice you recognize. It doesn't have to introduce itself. It feels predictable, even when it hurts. And for someone who learned early that safety was inconsistent, predictability, even painful predictability can feel like stability. I returned to the same emotional landscapes over and over, not because they were good for me, but because my nervous system knew how to navigate them. I knew where to stand, what to say, when to brace. I called that competence. It was conditioning.

Home, I learned, is not where you are most capable of surviving. It is where you are least required to armor yourself. That understanding came slowly, through moments that didn't match the old script. Conversations that didn't escalate. Silence that didn't threaten. Disagreements that ended in repair instead of withdrawal. At first, these moments felt foreign. My body waited for the crash that never came. My mind searched for the hidden cost. But over time, something inside me softened. The absence of danger began to feel real.

Letting go of familiar pain felt like grief. Not because I wanted the hurt, but because it meant releasing an identity I had built around endurance. I had been the one who could tolerate. The one who stayed calm under pressure. The one who didn't need much. Walking away from dynamics that hurt me meant admitting that strength is not measured by how much you can withstand. It is measured by how clearly you can choose what sustains you.

There were moments when the old pull returned. When I felt drawn toward people who mirrored past wounds, whose distance felt like a challenge, whose inconsistency activated something deep and practiced in me. But instead of romanticizing that pull, I paused. I asked different questions. Do I feel settled here, or just activated? Do I feel seen, or am I trying to be chosen?

Does this feel like connection, or like a test I already know how to take? Those questions became my compass. I began redefining home not as a place of intensity, but as a state of nervous system safety. Home became the space where my breath didn't shorten when someone took time to respond. Where my worth didn't fluctuate with attention. Where my needs didn't feel like liabilities. Home became where I could rest without fear of being forgotten, speak without rehearsing, exist without earning permission.

This shift changed how I moved through the world. I stopped chasing the familiar ache of almost-love. I stopped mistaking longing for depth. I stopped interpreting anxiety as chemistry. I learned that attraction rooted in unresolved pain feels urgent, consuming, and destabilizing. It keeps you reaching. Real connection, I discovered, feels grounding. It brings you back to yourself instead of pulling you away.

When I no longer mistook familiar pain for home, I didn't become numb. I became discerning. I didn't lower my capacity for love. I raised my standards for safety. I honored the part of me that had learned to survive by recognizing that survival is not the same as living. And for the first time, home stopped being something I searched for in other people.

It became something I carried—steady, quiet, and no longer built on pain.

Final Word

This book is not an accusation. It is not a defense. It is not an attempt to be forgiven, understood, or redeemed through language. It is a record. Of what was carried. Of what was broken. Of what was learned too late to save certain things, but not too late to save something else.

I did not write this to explain myself away. I wrote it to stop lying to myself.
There are losses that never fully heal. They do not resolve into lessons or transform neatly into gratitude. They simply remain quiet, heavy, and present. This is one of those losses. It did not end because love was absent. It ended because fear spoke louder than truth for too long. Because survival habits outpaced intimacy. Because patterns formed in pain were allowed to guide something that deserved steadiness instead.

Some of what was lost can never be restored. No amount of insight can return a life that required different timing, different tools, a different nervous system than the one I had then. Clarity does not reverse consequence. Awareness does not erase damage. And accepting that is part of the grief. Perhaps the hardest part.

There is sadness here, but not spectacle. Regret, but not self-punishment. Responsibility, without collapse. This is not the story of someone who didn't care. It is the story of someone who cared deeply but did not yet know how to stay fully present inside that care. And there is a difference.

If this book leaves anything behind, let it be this: understanding is not the same as absolution. Love is not the same as capacity. And healing is not a way back it is a way forward that does not pretend the past can be undone.

Some names will never be spoken again. Some rooms will remain out of reach. Some lives will continue without overlap. That is the cost. And it must be carried without dramatics, without bargaining, without distortion. Quietly. Honestly.

What remains is the responsibility to live differently, to choose presence over protection, to let fear be seen without letting it decide. Not to become perfect. Not to be free of loss. But to be awake.

This is not a closing of wounds. It is the closing of illusions. If there is any dignity left after loss, it is this: to tell the truth without asking it to save you, to hold what cannot be fixed without trying to justify it, and to keep going without turning away from what was lost.

This is where it ends. Not in resolution, but in clarity.